SINGERS

OF

DAYBREAK

Also by Houston A. Baker, Jr.

LONG BLACK SONG: *Essays in Black American Literature and Culture*

BLACK LITERATURE IN AMERICA (EDITOR)

TWENTIETH CENTURY INTERPRETATIONS OF *Native Son* (EDITOR)

SINGERS

OF

DAYBREAK

Studies in Black American Literature

Houston A. Baker, Jr.

HOWARD UNIVERSITY PRESS
WASHINGTON, D.C.
1983

Printed in the United States of America.

Library of Congress Cataloging in Publication Data

Baker, Houston A.
    Singers of daybreak.

    Bibliography: p.
    1. American literature—Afro-American authors—
History and criticism—Addresses, essays, lectures.
I. Title.
PS153.N5B27   1982   810'.9'896073   82–23280
ISBN 0–88258–017–5
ISBN 0–88258–025–6 (pbk.)

Acknowledgments

I AM grateful to the following publications for permission to reprint material that first appeared in their pages: *Black World* for "Paul Laurence Dunbar: An Evaluation" (November, 1971), " '*Utile Dulci*' and the Literature of the Black American" (September, 1972), "From the Inferno to the American Dream: George Cain's *Blueschild Baby*" (which appeared in the July, 1973, issue as a long review); *CLA Journal* for "The Achievement of Gwendolyn Brooks" (September, 1972); and *The Virginia Quarterly Review* for "A Forgotten Prototype: *The Autobiography of an Ex-Colored Man* and *Invisible Man*" (Summer, 1973). I also wish to thank Professor David Levin, who read a number of these essays in their early stages and suggested meaningful revisions, and Professor Arnold Rampersad who provided salient advice and an informative reading of the galleys. Of course, I extend my gratitude to my graduate assistant, Karen Kula, who worked faithfully on the bibliography. Finally, to my wife and my son go my sincere thanks for their patience and love.

To the Memory of
CHARLES A. WATKINS

Foreword

Wнy "singers of daybreak," when moral darkness covers the land and men speak words in the mourning time? The reasons are as simple as the implacable human will to survive and as complex as the multiform sensibility of the black writer in America, a man who still questions the paradox noted by Countee Cullen: "Yet do I marvel at this curious thing:/To make a poet black, and bid him sing!" But the moment of questioning is transformed into the words of the poem: the harps are retrieved from the willows and there follows a song of transcendence. Life renews itself, and a culture asserts its rejuvenation. We, thus, move from the nadir of the 1890s and the "Red Summer" of 1919 to the Harlem Renaissance. And after Till and Evers and Malcolm and King and so many more, we come to an era when men proclaim: "My blackness is the beauty of this land/my blackness/tender and strong, wounded and wise,/my blackness."

The essays that follow deal with several manifestations of the black creative spirit which have aided this process of cultural regeneration. They are concerned with writers, themes, and techniques that have helped to illumine the path for contemporaries and successors. James Weldon Johnson's *The Autobiography of an Ex-Colored Man,* for example, is analyzed as a prototype for Ralph Ellison's *Invisible Man.* The work of Paul Laurence Dunbar, the first black American poet of distinction, is re-evaluated, and the role of Jean Toomer's *Cane* in the black American artistic tradition is assessed, in the longest essay in the volume. Similarly, Gwendolyn Brooks's poetical stance; the topic of justice in the black narrative; George Cain's novel of inner-city life and drug addiction; and the issues raised by a consideration of entertainment and instruction as critical criteria provide content for essays and point to some of the more lustrous aspirations and achievements of black American culture.

It would be dishonest to place before the reader a more exact design, since each of the essays was written at a different time and seldom with others in view. The most obvious conjunction exists between the treatment of Johnson and Ellison and the essay "Black Culture, White Judgment: Patterns of Justice in the Black Narrative." Of course, there are also parallels between the careers of Dunbar and Brooks, and it is perhaps enlightening to juxtapose Toomer's lyrical presentation of early-twentieth-century black America with George Cain's portrayal of the contemporary black urban community. The concerns touched upon in " '*Utile Dulci*' and the Literature of the Black American" are general enough to affect each of the works and writers considered. Hence, this essay opens the volume.

I will not carry my disclaimer too far, however, because the subjects have a kind of unity in multiplicity. The works of Dunbar, Johnson, Toomer, Ellison, and Brooks have all been vital forces in the black American literary tradition, and justice for the black American has been a topic of ceaseless debate from 1619 to the present. *Blueschild Baby* is in some ways a summation of the synthesizing, creative impulses of the late 1960s, manifesting both the strengths and the shortcomings of that era. And the question of privileged criteria in the evaluation of black literature has loomed large since the turn of the century. The essays, therefore, might be regarded as delineations, even evocations, of those forces that have played an essential part in the well-being of a culture. They offer counterpoints in that rhythmical and anguished cycle of the black American by setting forth, or, better, by reflecting prismatically, the light that has been cast by our own singers of daybreak.

H.A.B.

University of Virginia
January 16, 1974

Introduction

SITTING at a large, antique table that might have appeared in any of Balzac's novels, I could hear in the mornings the soft chatter and restrained greetings of French men, women and children leaving the apartment complex to begin their day's activities. I had decided in 1972 that Paris was an ideal city in which to spend a university leave. A friend of mine in New York had a friend in Paris who was interested in renting his apartment for the spring semester. My family and I took up residence abroad in February. We have the usual hilarious stories of culture shock, settling in, getting accustomed to the people and botching the language. What is more pertinent, however, is the earnestness with which we approached our period of time abroad.

I had shipped ahead two enormous boxes of books, notes, papers, articles and jottings to be transformed, I hoped, into wise and finished critical reflections on Afro-American literature and culture. At that time, I used the term *black American* rather than *Afro-American*, and in a deadly earnest sense, I considered myself and my family part of a revolution in progress. Black Americans had demanded "Black Power," and many of us felt that the demand had been partially fulfilled. After all, there were now a host of new black enterprises. There were enough black intellectuals to justify a book describing their "crisis." The entertainment industry (especially the motion pictures) was characterized by an ever-spiralling number of black participants. Black students were a significant component of entering classes at traditionally all-white colleges and universities. Black politicians were a new and important southern and urban reality. And the list of manifestations of what some of us deemed a genuine increase in "Black Power" went on. There were new black publishing establishments, new journals and emergent groups of black creative artists and scholars such as the "Yardbird School" in California and the Organization of Black American Culture (OBAC) group in Chicago. On the East Coast alone it was possible to travel from Charlottesville, Virginia to New York, work at the Schomburg Collection in the company of twenty or thirty other scholars, catch a black play on Broadway, visit several black bookstores in Harlem, hear a black poetry reading, receive word of several black cultural festivals that were imminent, and return on a flight to Charlottesville with some well-known black intellectual or artist en route to a speaking engagement for the Black Studies program of the University of Virginia. Such were the black "contents" of the times in the United States in 1972.

My "wise and finished critical reflections" were to become part of this general (and, I felt, revolutionary) content destined to change the form of America in dramatic ways. For, once I had abandoned my graduate school plans to write definitive critiques of British Victorian literature and had turned to black American literature and culture, "cultural nationalism" became the ideologically-determined project in my intellectual life. My general goal—and that of others who populated the cultural nationalist camp—was to effect a cultural revolution, a general upheaval in traditional American conceptions of "the best" that had been thought and known in the world. Our project involved, first, an exposé of the exclusionary character of traditional American cultural agencies such as reviews, journals, mass media, schools and universities. We were intent on demonstrating that such agencies were devoted exclusively to the perpetuation of Anglo-American norms. We assumed that such an exposé would constitute a telling blow at the oft-heralded but seldom demonstrated plurality of what was called the "American cultural tradition." Our work would unequivocally demonstrate the hypocrisy of all claims to pluralism by the American cultural establishment and open the way for new entries into the cultural arena. These new entries were the second concern of our project. We were interested in bringing to light and promoting to a position of high cultural relevance, arts and artifacts deriving from an African heritage in America. In the streets, black people were proclaiming "Black is beautiful!" In our respective rented rooms, offices and studies, we were intent on demonstrating exactly the same point, under the rubric of the "aesthetic." If we could not begin with confident authority at the bronzes of Benin, we could, at least, turn to the brillance of Bearden, the books of Baldwin and the blues of Bessie. Yes, there was an immense legacy to be "retrieved," analyzed and promoted to prominence. The result of our labors, we felt, would be a confirmation—at an aesthetic and intellectual level—of the fact that black American culture was a separate and unique culture containing an accomplished repertoire of arts, artisans and artists.

The ancestral grounding of the cultural nationalist projects—the authenticating legacy which is required by every revolutionary movement to show its genuine connection with the mass life of the "nation"—was the Harlem Renaissance. The flowering of black creativity and criticism in the American 1920s was designated "Renaissance One"; our own era of the 1960s and 1970s was deemed a second renaissance. Collectively, the work of retrieval and original creativity of the earlier generation and of our own would present to the black American reflections of our beauty. The age, we proclaimed, demanded an image, a new and positive *image* of a black legacy that allowed for the existence of a unique black-American self.

LeRoi Jones, a founding member of the cultural nationalist camp, defined the cultural process in the following terms:

> What a culture produces, is, and refers to, is an image—a picture of a process, since it is a form of process: movement seen . . . Good-bad,

Beautiful-ugly, are all formed as the result of image. The mores, customs, of a place are the result of experience, and a common reference for defining it—common images.

What Jones captures in this statement (and in a host of similar statements in *Home* and *Raise Race Rays Raze*) is the man-made, or *symbolic*, nature of culture. From the chaotic world of nature, culture emerges by way of images. What one sees is a function of the codified modes of perception that one is taught. The cultural shorthand for these codified perceptual modes is the image or "cultural unit."

Culture is a collectivity of human beings bound by a shared symbolic discourse. Jones and others of the cultural nationalist camp felt that the primacy of the symbolic, particularly the linguistically symbolic, in the cultural enterprise gave special prominence to the articulate spokesperson or artist. "The Black Artist," wrote Jones, "must draw out of his soul the correct image of the world. He must use this image to bond his brothers and sisters together in common understanding of the nature of the world (and the nature of America) and the nature of the human soul." Culture reduced to image was, thus, two-fold: it exposed the actual nature of the world, and it provided a bonding for black men and women. Culture reduced to image was also viewed as a weapon that the black American spokesperson or artist employed to bring down the edifices of a traditional cultural establishment and to liberate black men and women from the tyranny of distorted images projected by that establishment. "The serious black artist of today," wrote Addison Gayle, Jr. in his 1971 introduction to *The Black Aesthetic*, "is at war with the American society as few have been throughout American history." It would not be amiss to add another combatant to the bellicose relationship projected by Gayle—the black American critic. For Gayle, like others in the cultural nationalist camp, certainly advocated the black critic's employment of culture-as-image-as-weapon to help "black people out of the polluted mainstream of Americanism."

The most trusted editor in the cultural nationalist camp was the late Hoyt W. Fuller, a man who transformed a second-rate digest into a lively journal of black art and culture. Those enlisted in the cultural nationalist cause knew that Hoyt Fuller would welcome their finished work and give them a place in his resonant *Black World*. I wrote to Fuller from Paris and told him of my plans for the year. I received in reply a magnificently encouraging note. I had all the encouragement a writer needed, and so I turned to my projected critical reflections with alacrity.

Unlike some of my predecessors who had gone to Paris, I regarded the city not as a haven from oppression, but as a romantic metropolis that Langston Hughes had taught me to see (in *The Big Sea*) in a peculiarly black American way. My emotional and intellectual centers were the heart of what I, along with others, thought of as a rising *nation* in the heart of America. I was not an alienated black American. My subject and subjectivity were indisputably fixed in black America.

It would be unfair, however, to minimize the power of some Parisian experiences. There were the massed, darkly-clad, helmeted French policemen who ringed "Paris VII" (one of the branches of the Sorbonne organized after the student uprisings of May, 1968) on the afternoon that I showed up to give a talk. "Paris VII" was unequivocally closed for the day as a result of "revolutionary" disturbances during the morning hours. The image I received was one of the Police State in confrontation with the Intellectuals. A few weeks later, I visited Vincennes, a "radical" branch of the University of Paris established after the fervor of May, 1968. The classrooms and corridors had been vandalized by the students. The closed-circuit television sets had been smashed, and across campus and within buildings there was an air of self-consumption. By superstition's acount, the hoop-snake devours itself—tail first. Having been granted a campus, French radicals had destroyed it in acts of "revolt."

But the negative images were countered by the kindness and contributions of professor Michel Fabre, whose apartment my family and I had rented. Fabre had been kind enough to leave not only his impressive collection of African, Caribbean and black American books, but also made available to me his many friends and colleagues directly involved in the study of black American literature and culture.

Fabre provided an international connection to the black experience that changed my conception of the overall dimensions of the cultural nationalist work that was to be done. He gave a global perspective to our labor. When I found the entire United States tucked neatly into a tiny corner of the Musee de l'Homme on a Sunday afternoon visit, I understood the importance of this global perspective.

And so, I sat at the antique, French table and wrote—with a sense of excitement, of eagerness and purpose, that was international in scope. I wrote essays on Jean Toomer's *Cane* and on the works of James Weldon Johnson and Ralph Ellison. I revised essays and read galley and page proofs for a book that I had completed the previous summer. The norm for the year was intense, intellectual effort devoted to a cause. My plan was to complete a book-length manuscript and dispatch it to the recently established Third World Press overseen by Don L. Lee, a founding member of OBAC.

I did, in fact, complete my manuscript by early summer of 1972, but by the time I had finished the work, Third World Press had decided to concentrate its efforts on social and political analyses. My manuscript was not suitable. Fortunately, the Howard University Press had come into being by 1973. I submitted *Singers of Daybreak* to Howard, and in June of 1973, I received word of its acceptance. It seemed singularly fitting that a book produced under the auspices of a cultural nationalist prospect should find a home at a new, black publishing establishment.

My leave in France was supported by the Center for Advanced Studies at the University of Virginia, and I returned to a post in the English department there. In the humid summer of 1973, therefore, I was a cultural nationalist situated at a university that had traditionally been all-male, all-white and more-than-mildly (as one soon learned) pro-Confederate. The financing for my "revolutionary" intellectual labors was a devastatingly ironic function of Anglo-America. Both "Paris VII" and Vincennes have returned to mind on more than one occasion.

Introduction

I was not exactly akin to the self-consuming hoop-snake, or the feckless intellectual "closed" down by a powerful state, but I was certainly a person whose labors had been duly considered (by the State, as it were) and processed. What I want to suggest here is that a containment of black American cultural nationalism was powerfully operative in the very year, 1973, that *Singers of Daybreak* was guaranteed publication. The strategies of containment, however, did not, in the final analysis, deserve that name. For no one in Anglo-America had actually devoted a great deal of conscious thought to eradicating or containing a cultural nationalist project. Certainly, many Anglo-Americans detested the exposé of their various hypocrises effected by cultural nationalism, and they despised the idea of a "black presence" in a traditionally all-white academy. But, in truth, most academicians are so wedded to their intellectual labors and so intent on separating intellection from action that they rarely get around to doing anything about their beliefs, assertions, claims or hypotheses. Hence, innuendo, snide comments and "liberal demurrers" are the ways of the academy.

Very few academicians had the courage in the liberal 1960s to come out and attack cultural nationalism in direct, unequivocal terms. Instead, they relied on what LeRoi Jones has described as "Black compradors" to do the job. These black American opportunists—who had consciously accepted their inferior status vis-a-vis Anglo-America (i.e., who had wholeheartedly accepted the criteria of intellectual excellence of a racialistic Anglo-American society)—were encouraged to condemn cultural nationalism with all the resources at their disposal. Vincennes comes sadly to mind. What Anglo-America did, in effect, was confine all black intellectuals to a single arena by offering a small number of academic posts for occupancy and by encouraging blacks to make their own bellicose bids for these positions. Ralph Ellison, with his characteristic brilliance, has raised the ritual represented by this Anglo-American mode of operation to high art in the "battle royal" scene of his *Invisible Man.* Blindfolded, and egged on by Anglo-Americans, blacks battled one another for academic advantage. Realizing their opportunity to become spokespersons on literature and art at full salary, many were easily persuaded to participate in the slugfest that brought cultural nationalism to a dreary impasse, to a defensive posture in which the enemy was no longer conceived as white, cultural imperialism, but as black "revolutionary nationalism," "Marxism," "Neo-Hoodooism," and so on. Today, the results of this battle can be viewed as a split decision. On one side are the "tough idealists" who somehow survived the embattlement of their adversaries, while on the other, are the compradors who led the assault on cultural nationalism for the white academy. Representatives of both groups have found niches in the American academy. And in that academy today, a romantically idealistic cultural nationalism no longer seems a viable intellectual posture.

If I were commencing my labors today, I would scarcely produce *Singers of Daybreak*. This judgment does not imply, however, that cultural nationalism was without virtue. One of the singular benefits of that project was its success in promoting black American culture to the status of an "academically respectable" subject for study. In a sense, it gave a local habitation and a name to an enterprise that currently provides work for a large group of American scholars. Within this group of "Afro-Americanists" are literary analysts who are dedicated to describing the uniqueness of black American literature in rigorously theoretical terms.

One might consider the movement that has carried black American literary study from cultural nationalist *assertions* to literary-theoretical *descriptions* as a progression toward the mainstream. But a second benefit of the cultural nationalist project was its iconoclasm; one which shattered traditional verities with brash confidence and provided conditions of existence for a radically modified establishment. A concern for literary theory—for modes of explanation and analysis that account for a variety of texts—is but one academic manifestation of this drastically altered establishment. As new and different expressive products were introduced into the academy, new modes of study were required.

The present edition of *Singers of Daybreak* will enter a universe of literary–theoretical study that it, in some ways, helped to foster. One of the signal aspects of this universe of discourse is that it contains among its spokespersons a number of "singers of day-break." Today, there are no French voices drifting to me as the day's activities begin. Instead, there are the well-thought questions posed by my eleven-year-old son. "What," he asked recently, "are singers of daybreak?" "They are," I responded, "Black men and women who will not allow Anglo-America to control their voices." To such "singers" in the contemporary world of Afro-American literary study, I dedicate this present edition of *Singers of Daybreak*.

Philadelphia, Pennsylvania
January 19, 1982   H.A.B.

Contents

SINGERS OF DAYBREAK

We are not come to wage a strife
With swords upon this hill
It is not wise to waste the life
Against a stubborn will

Yet would we die as some have done
Beating a way for the rising sun.

—ARNA BONTEMPS

I

"Utile Dulci" and the Literature
of the Black American

IN *Novelists on the Novel* (London: Routledge and Kegan Paul, 1965), Miriam Allott asserts that "in general, the novelist's desire to emphasize the *utile* at the expense of the *dulce* has usually had damaging effects on his adjustment of 'the uncommon' and 'the ordinary,' interfering with the effect of verisimilitude which it is important for him to achieve and also impairing his purity of vision" (p. 30). One reaction to such a statement is concurrence; another is that Miss Allott has not presented a just distinction. In fact, there never has been a distinction between the *utile* and the *dulce*, the didactic and the amusing, in art, and such a neat bifurcation is unlikely to occur in the foreseeable future. The new critics of twentieth-century Britain and America worked assiduously to prove that the successfully completed work of art was an organic whole embodying its own set of attitudes and assumptions and divorced from the values of the author and the rude touch of sociology and history. The art-for-art's-sake writers and critics of nineteenth-century France and England had taken an even more extreme position: completed works become *émaux et camées*—precious, lapidary artifacts free of didacticism. One supposes that Miss Allott—like so many who have suffered their influence—has the critical canons of these two groups in mind when she speaks of an infringing *utile* and its corruption of a "pure" artistic vision. Moreover, her statement might be accepted as a sort of metaphysical *donnée* by the fiercely anti-puritan mind that has been nurtured on the decline of vital moral authority witnessed by our century. If God is dead then everything is possible; more importantly, if God is dead then there is no great providential scheme for the artist to reflect, and he must satisfy the hungry, questing, intellectual soul of his readers by becoming a god unto himself, dispensing the doctrine and dogma of art—the new religion. Hence the need for "purity of vision" on the part of the artist, a need to tune his instruments finely and steer a skillful course between *utile* and *dulce*.

In fact, the process has been weighted heavily in favor of *dulce*, and the implication that there are twin dangers equal in the censure they have received is somewhat misleading. Few people revel in the finger-pointing and scathing denunciation of the preacher; many, on the other hand, are willing to accept mindless pleasure. In short, a work that is all didacticism would be immediately rejected by the anti-puritans, while a work that was all entertainment would receive critical upbraiding by the highly serious but in the end might be exonerated on the grounds that it gave pleasure to the "uninformed." But even here the dichotomy is not just, because our definitions of didacticism and entertainment have a way of becoming entangled.

The process of categorization usually involves some arbitrariness, and the more generalized and inclusive the category, the less serviceable it is in the office of precise definition. Both *utile* and *dulce* have suffered from the vagueness of categorization. If a work entertains us sufficiently, it falls into the latter class, regardless of its preaching and polemics. If we are not amused, the work falls in the former division, despite the fact that (as British critics phrase it) "it contains some terribly entertaining scenes." And strategic literary questions either remain unanswered or receive a response that accords with the whim of the critic. Is *Moby Dick*, for example, a tome of *ex cathedra* transcendental preaching or a thrilling adventure of the whaling industry? Is William Styron's *The Confessions of Nat Turner* a meditation (in the firmest Loyolan sense of the word) on

[2]

history or a pleasurable throwback to the Plantation Tradition? To insist that the works are perfect blends of **utile** and **dulce** is to avoid the issue, since Melville is clearly more self-consciously polemical than Styron, and Styron is not entertaining at all to the informed black American reader.

In the manner of most white Western categories, those of **utile** and **dulce** have militated against black American literature and culture. Very few works in the black American literary tradition have been considered fine enough combinations of the two categories to receive even faint praise. In general, works by black American authors have been considered excessively didactic, and when they have been acknowledged for their utilitarian quality, white critics have felt compelled to point out that such **utile** has been purchased "at the expense of the **dulce**." Black authors have faced continually the type of criticism that Irving Howe levels at Richard Wright. Howe first asserts that a black American author can fulfill his calling only if he protests loud and long against the injustices suffered by his people; next he praises Wright for following his true calling. But according to Howe any writer who protests too long and too loudly is guilty of excessive preaching; hence, he labels *Native Son*, one of the finest novels ever produced in America, a crude book. Howe's criticism and that of other white scholars such as Robert Bone, Theodore Gross, and David Littlejohn leave little doubt in the mind of a black reader that the odds and the categories have been stacked against him. Most American critics have not felt that the sermons of the Mathers and Jonathan Edwards, the poetry of Anne Bradstreet, Michael Wigglesworth, and Edward Taylor, or the scurrilous opuses of Benjamin Franklin and Henry Adams were excessively didactic. What is one to make, then, of their condemnation of David Walker, Richard Wright, Imamu Amiri Baraka, and Don L. Lee? One can, I think, make a case for the rather obvious fact that literature and ideology, criticism and ideology, have never existed as separate entities.

Jonathan Edwards, Edward Taylor, Benjamin Franklin, and most of the other white authors who find a place on American literature syllabi, have shared the *sui generis* assumptions of those tattered pilgrims and convicted felons who made their way to this

[3]

country and proclaimed "an errand into the wilderness" as justification for slaughtering the natives and enslaving millions. True, their writings sometimes go against the American grain, but time and again they reaffirm the great promise of manifest destiny: what Sartre calls that "proud security and that tranquil certainty, common to all white Aryans, that the world is white and that they own it." The American ideology—the documents that undergird the republic and the ideas that reflect its needs and aspirations—has excluded a consideration of blacks as human beings. And American literature and criticism—those luminous cultural mirrors—have done the same. What lies behind the neglect of black American literature is not a supportable body of critical criteria that includes a meaningful definition of *utile* and *dulce* but a refusal to believe that blacks possess the humanity requisite for the production of works of art. This is, indeed, an incongruous situation; it is, as Addison Gayle has stated it, "the black situation."

Black Americans have always looked upon the American experience from a perspective of incongruity. White Americans have designated the black cultural experience an abyss without the Nietzchean awareness that "if you gaze long into an abyss, the abyss will gaze back into you." Manifest destiny, the inalienable rights of man, an errand into the wilderness, what had these to do with black Americans? David Walker saw them as justifications for avarice and predicted a frightening apocalypse that would cleanse the earth of its white oppressors. Frederick Douglass viewed them as rationalizations for the evil of slavery. And long before either Douglass or Walker, the southern, agrarian black folk had seen them as the comic palliatives that whites used in order to sleep at night; Br'er Rabbit launches more than one frontal assault on that "tranquil certainty" of Br'er Bear and Br'er Fox. Martin Delany, in *Blake or the Huts of the Americas*, defines the errand into the wilderness as the stealthy travels of his own protagonist through the American South, inciting insurrection and calling for the violent overthrow of the enslavers. And in Charles Chesnutt's novels and short stories, the manifest destiny of the white American is to suffer sorrow, misfortune, disappointment, and a frightening naivety as the natural results of his capitalistic treks into the wilderness. In short, what I have elsewhere called "an index of repudiation" characterizes the black American literary tradition; the ideology of white America is rejected and replaced by a celebration of the communality, survival values, and richness of the black American cultural experience. What one has is neither protest nor excessive didacticism but the simple and eloquent fact of black American humanity in its manifold dimensions. And it is precisely the black American's humanity that white America has never been able to concede. Thus a literary tradition that commences with an accomplished folk base and spans three centuries has been written off under the heading of *utile*. The irony, of course, is that any author who sits down to write has a very utilitarian purpose in mind; he wishes to instill an ideology, even if it is the ideology that art "must not mean but be." Théophile Gautier, after all, was one of the most ideological artists in the history of French literature, and his pure and gemlike poems rest on volumes of morality. It is not the polemics of black literature that worries the white American critic; he is used to that if he is at all familiar with his own literary tradition. What bothers him is the possibility that when he shouts menacingly into the abyss, "I know you are down there," the answer will come back "Ah, but I am!"

Commenting on the blindness of his white characters in *Native Son*, Richard Wright said that the one thing that would have solved the murder mystery of the novel within a half hour was missing—an acknowledgment of Bigger Thomas's humanity by one, or all, of the white investigators. Wright's statement helps to solve the "mystery" of the missing black American literature in the writings and on the syllabi of white American scholars. The frank and unequivocal acknowledgment of the black man's humanity holds as a corollary a certain degree of intellectual curiosity, a desire to analyze and understand the unique aspects of his culture and to study the answers he has offered to the timeless problems of the universe. The charge of *utile* will no longer suffice. The didactic component of black American literature is no more grating to the ears of white American critics than the utilitarian sermonizing on an errand into the wilderness, the inalienable rights of man, and the quest for a new frontier to the ears of black critics. The ideological component of art is part

[5]

of its *raison d'être,* and only those who deceive themselves in the manner of Miss Allott can believe that it somehow encroaches on a more important element and distorts verisimilitude and pure artistic vision. The verisimilitude of a work of art is always contingent on the informed reader's conception of reality, and it is the extent to which the author's vision corresponds to the reader's conception that determines the accuracy of his work. The nearer the artist is to the people, the greater will be his chance of giving a just description of reality. Miss Allott, the art-for-art's-sake school, and the new critics have attempted to make art a closed circle for the intelligentsia, and when the warm touch of humanity or the "engaged" voice of the artist who defines his task as the liberation of men and the satisfaction of the needs of free men confronts them, they cry out: "That is not it at all,/That is not what I meant at all." But this is decidedly what black American critics of this era mean. There has always been a host of ideologies competing, combining, and conflicting in an attempt to gain the ear of art, but there never has been and never will be an essential distinction between *utile* and *dulce.* And today's black American authors and critics have taken up the struggle where the last generation left off. They have found it necessary to question seriously the chameleon terminology of the white critical establishment, which means one thing when applied to Ralph Waldo Emerson and quite another when applied to Ralph Waldo Ellison, and they have insisted that art exists for one reason only —to serve the people who provide its symbols and values.

II

Black Culture, White Judgment:
Patterns of Justice in the Black Narrative

Widespread legal control of the black man was the function of eighteenth-century American slave codes. The codes, according to one historian, constituted a "public dialogue among masters and among white men generally, intended to confirm their sense of mastery over their Negro slaves—and over themselves."[1] Starting with negative identification—the definition of oneself by what one must never become (heathen, savage, barbaric, black, or red)— white colonialists proceeded to codify their fears and their exploitation of human resources. One had to keep his black property in check or the entire system might fall apart. If the oppressive center would not hold, if white men could not restrain the barbarian within their midst, then not only the plantation economy but also the moral order that had been so laboriously imposed upon the lands of the new world would be destroyed.

Like a papal bull of old, the word went forth. It was preached from pulpits, presented at town meetings, mused over, debated, and finally—always—accepted at elaborate social gatherings of white masters and their associates. *The black man is the beast in our newly found jungle*. And here the allusion is not accidental. One critic has

[7]

said that Henry James writes blank checks for evil that we fill in with evil of our own devising. The white American situation—contingent upon an African slave trade, the brutalization of blacks, and rampant economic exploitation—offered such a blank check, and whites filled in the line marked culpability with a distorted image of the black American. The image was as much a psychological construct as the fearful beast in James's story, and its effects have been just as devastating. White Americans were imprisoned by their own fantasies and projections, while blacks—deemed beyond the pale of a Christian and reasonable humanity—became the incarcerated labor force of America.

Booker T. Washington succinctly captures the nature of white cultural assumptions when he writes: "No white American ever thinks that any other race is wholly civilized until he wears the white man's clothes, eats the white man's food, speaks the white man's language, and professes the white man's religion."[2] And though W. E. B. Du Bois pointed out in *Dusk of Dawn* that "it is only possible for the white race to prove its own incontestable superiority by appointing both judge and jury and summoning its own witnesses,"[3] when the white court is the only one available, that "superiority" can seem unassailable. Moreover, in such a situation, the possibility of exoneration or acquittal seems remote indeed. A black folktale, "Ole Sis Goose," expresses most clearly what I am trying to get at here:

Ole Sis Goose wus er-sailing' on de lake, and ole Br'er Fox wus hid in de weeds. By um by ole Sis Goose swum up close to der bank and ole Br'er Fox lept out an cotched her.

"O yes, ole Sis Goose, I'se got yer now, you'se been er-sailin' on der lake er long time, en I'se got yer now. I'se gwine to break yer neck en pick yer bones."

"Hole on der', Br'er Fox, hold on, I'se got jes' as much right to swim in der lake as you has ter lie in der weeds. Hit's des' as much my lake as hit is yours, and we is gwine to take dis matter to der cotehouse and see if you has any right to break my neck and pick my bones."

And so dey went to cote, and when dey got dere, de sheriff, he wus er fox, and de judge, he wus er fox, and der tourneys, dey wus fox, en all de jurymen, dey was foxes too.

En dey tried ole Sis Goose, en dey 'victed her and dey 'scuted her, and dey picked her bones.

Now, my chilluns, listen to me, when de folks in de cotehouse is foxes,

and you is des' er common goose, der ain't gwine to be much justice for
you pore cullud folks.[4]

The judgment of the foxes in a world where foxes are in power is no
more surprising than the judgment bestowed upon the lion by the
hunter who writes the story. "But this," the father told an inquisitive
child, who wondered why the "king of beasts" was always the loser
in jungle stories, "will change when lions learn to write." The question posed here is, Did the situation change when black Americans
began to write their own story? What ramifications of the white
world's judgment, in short, are to be observed in that most telling
social mirror, black American literature? The answer implies a concern with the concept of justice and the norms to be found in the
literature, and an examination of several representative narratives
leads to certain tentative conclusions.

II

One of the most notable aspects of the black narrative tradition
is the condition of limitation with which many of its works begin. We
do not find the classical paradigm of exalted position, followed by a
fateful act or choice leading to a fall. Nor do we have that archetypal
"U," which carries the comic action from an optimistic plane through
the slough of despond and back to the peaks of harmony. The initial
state in the black narrative is usually one of bondage, imprisonment,
or circumscription—either physical or mental, or both together—and
the pattern of action involves an attempt to break out of this narrow
arena. The final state, however, is seldom one that encompasses an
ideal freedom; often it is an admixture of hope and despair, concilia-
tion and implacability, madness and sanity, repleteness and longing.
The *Narrative of the Life of Frederick Douglass, An American Slave,
Written by Himself* (1845)[5] offers a case in point.

One of the chief motivations for the *Narrative* was Douglass's
desire to convince the doubtful that he had been a slave, but a careful
look at the versions of self shows that more was involved than crafting
an affidavit. From the simple, descriptive opening statements to the
appendix, there is a strict autobiographical pattern at work. The author is concerned to show how a black man situated in what was

commonly known during the nineteenth century as "the prison house of slavery" made his way to the North and the abolitionist movement. The initial condition is one of bondage, deprivation, and injustice. The young Douglass does not know his father, and he sees his mother only two or three times before she dies. His life is free of specific tasks but always subject to the whims of his owners. And he is confronted early on by the nakedness of the white man's personal power, for he sees his Aunt Hester savagely and unjustly whipped, and he watches in awful horror as a white overseer shoots the slave Demby, "without consultation or deliberation with any one." The young boy is told that he is to be sent to Baltimore to care for one of his master's relatives. He has no choice in the matter, and, though he is happy to leave the plantation, he can assign no reason for his having been sent.

In Baltimore he witnesses a neighbor's cruelty to her slaves, and after he has been given the barest rudiments of education by his white mistress, he comes abruptly in contact with the white world's conception of the black man. Mr. Auld tells his wife that education will ruin the best black servant and that she must never again endeavor to instruct Douglass. This is a revelation for both the mistress and the slave. Mrs. Auld moves rapidly toward the white consensus; she becomes aware of her personal power and begins to treat the slave in a manner befitting her race. Douglass, on the other hand, sees his master's injunction as exactly the knowledge he needs. He now knows his status in the world and begins to understand the strategies he must employ if he wishes to move beyond his initial condition. The remainder of the *Narrative* traces the self's successive movements through the roles of trickster, badman, educated leader, and intelligent rebel.

It is only by setting himself psychologically apart from the larger society that Douglass is able to achieve his victory. He places himself (paradoxically) in an extralegal position in order to obtain justice. This stance allows him to see the world around him as it really is, and he discovers that the "soul-killing" power of slavery has reduced practically every white person to a hypocritical brute. His experiences with Mr. Covey, the slavebreaker, and Thomas Auld, the master, offer a climactic point in the *Narrative* and are representative of the work's patterns of justice.

While aiding in the fanning of wheat, Douglass falls sick. Mr. Covey refuses to believe that he is ill, and, after giving him a savage kick and a heavy blow with a hickory slat, he leaves the young slave to his fate. Douglass decides to seek redress from his master, and he walks seven miles to Thomas Auld's house and presents himself in a sad and bloody condition. The master hears the case and renders his judgment:

> Master Thomas ridiculed the idea that there was any danger of Mr. Covey's killing me, and said that he knew Mr. Covey, that he was a good man, and that he could not think of taking me from him; that, should he do so, he would lose the whole year's wages; that I belonged to Mr. Covey for one year, and that I must go back to him, come what might; and that I must not trouble him with any more stories, or that he would himself *get hold of me.* (Pp. 79-80)

There seems no recourse, not even God, since both Auld and Covey are professing Christians, and Douglass must turn elsewhere. He yields to superstition by taking a protective root from Sandy Jenkins, then chooses physical force as his most effective means of resistance. He assumes the role of the badman hero as he wrestles the slave-breaker to the ground, escapes whipping, and resolves that henceforth "the white man who expected to succeed in whipping, must also succeed in killing me." It is but a short step from this resolution to Douglass's decision to make a bid for freedom. As the educated and determined leader of Mr. Freeland's slaves, he sets the course, and though his first venture is unsuccessful, he soon tries again and gains the North.

The pattern of action that concludes with Douglass's escape begins with Mr. Auld's caution. It is the slave's expanding awareness of the exclusiveness of white justice that leads to subtle rebellion, physical revolt, and finally a departure from the system. It is only through the careful autobiographical structuring of the *Narrative,* however, that Douglass emerges as a determined and heroic figure. Repeatedly, one sees the agony and uncertainty the initial condition produces; at Mr. Covey's, the protagonist is reduced to an almost total impercipience: "I was broken in body, soul, and spirit. My natural elasticity was crushed, my intellect languished, the disposition to read departed, the cheerful spark that lingered about my eye died; the dark night of slavery closed in upon me; and behold a man transformed into a brute!" (p. 75). And on his arrival in New York, Douglass is still unsure of himself and fearful of the omnipresent threat of captivity. He changes his name in order to avoid the thoroughgoing justice of the white world and is forced to move to Massachusetts before he feels somewhat secure. His actions are scarcely those of a man who has obtained an ideal state of freedom. They are rather those of the convicted felon, and even in Massachusetts he seems almost compelled to demonstrate that he is really safe. He recounts a long story of a former traitor and *soi-disant* slavecatcher who has been driven from the community like Beelzebub before the vengeful host. Finally, Douglass seems to feel that his only real sanctuary resides in the abolitionist movement: the entire system must change before he can be free. It is the demand of this agency that calls forth the *Narrative* itself, and it is the necessity to show the movement grounded in some larger ontological design (a true Christianity) that brings about the concluding apologia. The *Narrative*, therefore, is not only an autobiographical chronicle but also an act of freedom. It extends Douglass's abolitionist activities and offers a definition of liberating values. The telling of the tale creates freedom for both the narrator and his audience.

The *Narrative of the Life of Frederick Douglass* is one of the most accomplished of the innumerable accounts of black American slaves, and it is prototypical in the black narrative tradition. The pattern of justice and the movement of the protagonist in the *Narrative* are paradigmatic for such later works as James Weldon Johnson's *The Autobiography of an Ex-Colored Man* (1912), Richard Wright's *Native Son* (1940), Ralph Ellison's *Invisible Man* (1952), and *The Autobiography of Malcom X* (1964). Wright's Bigger Thomas, for example, moves outward from an initially circumscribed position. Incarcerated in the ghetto of Chicago, he longs for flight, to soar upward like the beautiful pigeon or to sail through the heavens like the silver advertising plane he sees at the book's opening. Staring him ominously in the face, however, is the billboard with the white State's Attorney's face and pointing finger; the caption reads, "If you break the law, you can't win."

Bigger, fascinated by the power of the white world, bombarded by distorted projections of communism and Africa, uncomprehending before the sociological jargon of Mrs. Dalton, and overwhelmed by the incongruous overtures of Mary and Jan, strikes out in terror at that most vulnerable nerve of American society— the white woman. He presses the pillow firmly over Mary's face as the spectral, white, and all too substantial Mrs. Dalton moves toward him. Bigger knows that to be discovered in the secret corridors of the white world is tantamount to death. In effect, the shadow from the abyss—from the depths of the white American mind—has leaped forward and destroyed the heiress designate, and Bigger now stands outside the patterns of justice defined by the surrounding society. The second part of *Native Son* is entitled "Flight."

The protagonist begins to understand the limitations imposed on him by the white world, and he plays the role of trickster and badman in order to avoid capture. The climax comes when he has scaled the grandest physical height he is to attain; from atop the water tower, he fires through the freezing cold at a mob that has come to take his life. Of course, Wright pictures Bigger in this concluding scene as a Christ figure; "two men stretched his arms out, as though about to crucify him." But Bigger is more than some divinity *manqué*.

The third section of the novel, "Fate," traces his expanding consciousness and gives us the most symbolic setting imaginable, a cramped jail cell. He has exchanged the ghetto for the jail, the image of the State's Attorney for the man himself, but he has also stood outside the world that attempts to hold him in fee. Slowly, agonizingly, he moves toward that state of resolution that characterizes Douglass after his encounter with Mr. Covey. Though he is confronted by the set ideological patterns of the priest, the preacher, and the communist lawyer, Bigger chooses a position that places him firmly outside the existing framework. Humanism may be inherent in his final stance, but only insofar as we are convinced that existentialism is a humanism.[6] Bigger decides that what he killed for "must have been good," that his extralegality was necessary, given the state of his

[13]

existence. He does not expect the white world to temper its justice with mercy, and he finds himself alone. He knows, however, that an understanding of the human situation—in this case, the black situation —makes it less difficult to die alone, and he smiles a faint, wry, bitter smile at the back of his retreating lawyer.

The Autobiography of an Ex-Colored Man and *Invisible Man* are so close in form and thematic development that the earlier work may be deemed a model for the later. Any written narrative by a black American might be considered an extralegal document, since the laws of the land prevented the education of slaves, and the history of American education, which is currently evolving under the heading "school desegregation," has been fiercely racialistic. *The Autobiography of an Ex-Colored Man* and *Invisible Man*, however, like Douglass's *Narrative*, are extralegal records of experience because their narrators stand, from the beginning, outside the patterns of white American justice. Douglass is a fugitive slave; Johnson's narrator is passing for white, and Ellison's invisible man is not only drawing power secretly from the white world but has also committed an assault on one of its citizens. The patterns of action in both Johnson's and Ellison's novels involve movement in a circular path where the respective protagonists come face to face with the meaning of white justice. For the ex-colored man, a brutal lynching serves the same function as the early views of slavery and Mr. Auld's injunction to his wife in the *Narrative of the Life of Frederick Douglass*. And in *Invisible Man* a long series of dehumanizing experiences leads to the realization that one must plunge outside the white man's history. In the end, Johnson's narrator finds himself in an alien world; he is a black man seizing the rewards of white society due to the accident of skin color, and at one point in the novel he sees himself akin to the un-found-out criminal. Of course, the invisible man is in a similar position. He inhabits a dark hole in a basement (one that has been shut off since the nineteenth century, implying that American attitudes were then more liberal), and though he talks of coming up to play a socially responsible role, one suspects that he has gained all of the accountability and freedom that are possible.

Finally, there is *The Autobiography of Malcolm X,* a book that

[14]

reads on one level like a paradigm of the American dream. Genea-
logically, it belongs with the tales of Benjamin Franklin and Horatio
Alger. To stop here, however, is to miss much of the work's essential
dynamism. Though Malcolm starts from a small town in Michigan
and makes his way to Boston, New York, and eventually the world,
his autobiography is more than the traditional success story filled
with improving maxims. The principal alliance in the book is always with black American culture, specifically the whole way of
life that characterizes the black inner city. *The Autobiography of
Malcolm X* delineates the movement from an agrarian to an urban
setting as equivalent to a descent into hell, and while a number of
other classic American works evince this same pattern, few do so
with the towering sense of moral rage that characterizes Malcolm's work—a rage predicated upon the racist history of the country at large. The message is not that "getting and spending, we lay
waste our powers," but rather that the white man has locked the
black man in an oppressive physical and psychological cage
and attempted to impose on him values and standards that destroy
his life.

The initial condition, therefore, is one of incarceration: "The
white man's heaven is the black man's hell." It is in prison that Malcolm—like Bigger Thomas—becomes fully aware of the truth of this
phrase and converts to the Islamic faith. The father of his new country
is not the archetypal white founding father or the blond heavenly
Patron but a small, brown-skinned man who preaches a doctrine
of separatism. Malcolm becomes a fisher of men in the country's
black ghettoes.

Having heard and witnessed the storm of abuse that greeted the
man when he was living and the innuendoes that surround the dead
leader's memory, one is probably not far afield if one says that in the
mind of many white Americans the name Malcolm X and the word
"criminality" are synonymous. Malcolm's expanding consciousness
pushed him beyond white Christianity and the brainwashed psyche
of the black hustler to the preachings of the Black Muslim movement. Finally, he had to stand outside even this, seeking a firm
orthodoxy at the *Ka'ba* itself and dying beyond the rigid codes
on either side of the American veil. His final stance, as Alex Haley

[15]

sketches it in the Epilogue, seems as devoid of a priori values as Bigger Thomas's.

III

In the black narrative, the judgment rendered by the white world manifests itself in a pattern of extralegality. Moving from an initially limited position, the black protagonist often finds himself outside the dictates of a society that attempts to confine him, and his expanding consciousness leads to the realization that it is not humanism or moral righteousness that brings about the adverse rulings of the white world, but a quest for personal power and a desire for psychological stability purchased at the price of a distorted image of the black American. Once the protagonist has moved beyond the limits of his society, however, he is not assured freedom. According to the standards of the world he has rejected, he is a criminal. The shades of the prison house are likely to close at any moment, and a renewed captivity is always imminent. At times, this makes the final position seem almost as circumscribed as the initial one.

The image of Sisyphus forcing his massive boulder uphill only to have it roll rapidly down again comes to mind, but if Camus is correct,[7] there is an instant between the momentary stasis at the top and the beginning of the descent in which something heroic occurs. One can assert, therefore, that the final positions of Frederick Douglass, Bigger Thomas, Johnson's and Ellison's narrators, and Malcolm X carry us toward a more elevated conception of the human condition. We have not only the insights and the liberating strategies that illuminate the course of the narration but also the honest complexity of endings that indicate no solution is final until the basis of the white court's power has been destroyed. The black narrative does not offer a comfortable majority report. It speaks of the enduring struggle of those who have been severely judged and restricted and yet have sought to evolve humane standards of existence. There is angst involved, but ultimately the process augurs well for some essential— perhaps an innate—human dignity.

[16]

III

A Forgotten Prototype: *The Autobiography of an Ex-Colored Man* and *Invisible Man*

THE process of literary comparison is, at best, demanding, for one quickly realizes that fundamental differences exist between any two works of art. To attempt to eradicate these distinctions is folly, and a struggle to fuse basically irreconcilable works into the same mold is an engaging task only for a latter-day Sisyphus. Northrop Frye is surely correct, however, when he says, "It [criticism] is knowledge that connects one experience with another, corrects false impressions and inadequacies, and makes possible that progression and sequence in experience without which there could be no such thing as criticism."[1] Hence, one can exercise restraint and still find grounds within the dynamics of criticism for discussing simultaneously James Weldon Johnson's *The Autobiography of an Ex-Colored Man* (1912) and Ralph Ellison's *Invisible Man* (1952).

Professor Woodridge, one of the minor characters in *Invisible Man*, says:

Stephen's [Dedalus's] problem, like ours, was not actually one of creating the uncreated conscience of his race, but of creating the *uncreated features of his face*. Our task is that of making ourselves individuals. The conscience of a race is the gift of its individuals who see,

[17]

evaluate, record. . . . We create the race by creating ourselves and then
to our great astonishment we will have created something far more important: We will have created a culture. Why waste time creating a conscience for something that doesn't exist? For, you see, blood and skin do
not think!"[2]

These lines contain a just assessment of the task of the black
American author, and they speak volumes about his literary tradition. The black man subjected to the rigors of the slave trade,
"broken" in the West Indies, and set to work in the rural South
among members of tribes whose languages he did not understand
found himself in a cultural void. His descendants—their African
family ties destroyed and they themselves graced with the first
classical, biblical, or humorous epithet that came to the master's
mind—found themselves not only in a cultural but also in a nameless void; they became Colonel Tyler's people, Little Liza's Jane,
Cato, Jeremiah, or Sunshine. WHAT IS YOUR NAME? the doctors
demand of Ellison's protagonist, and, like his African ancestors, he
is unable to answer the question with confidence. The task of the
black American author has been one of "creating the uncreated
features of his face" in order to move beyond the nameless abyss
in which all black Americans at one time or another find themselves. Though black authors cannot be readily equated with the
romantic poet's "unacknowledged legislators of the world," they
can be identified as culture builders and historians of a distinctive,
whole way of life.

The enforced conformity of the black American experience is
one of the facts of American history that is often obscured by a
veil of clichés and half-truths. One realizes, however, that the
American holders of power (and race theorizers in their employ)
have generally defined all black men in the same manner: inferior,
bound by no rights a white man need respect, and objects for inhumane treatment. Paradoxically, this American racism provided
a basis for a separate and distinctive black American culture and
brought about a synonymity in the perspectives of black Americans.
A slave in rural Georgia, for example, was likely to have more in
common with one in the industrial North than two nineteenth-century white merchants living on the east and west sides of New York.

The country at large had defined the condition of the slaves and dedicated itself to their mortification; the businessmen, on the other hand, served different clienteles and had different assumptions for the conduct of life, though both had every right to share the omnipresent and indefatigable myth of the American frontier. The white world of possibility faced a proscriptive black world where the prime issue was survival. This clarifies the generative conditions of the black American author. As the writer struggled to overcome his limitations—to elucidate his own situation and move toward a sense of personal identity—he undertook the same task for the group as a whole, since it was bound by the same conditions. The foundation in criticism for discussing the works of Johnson and Ellison together resides within a specific cultural context. William Fischer points out, for example, that the heroes of novels go unnamed through a series of incidents containing "various typical features of black life in America,"[3] and this, combined with similar aspects of *The Autobiography of an Ex-Colored Man* and *Invisible Man*, reinforces what is here a basic assumption: that a reader loses more by ignoring an important prototype for Ellison's novel than he gains from the sum of the highly ingenious, structuralist commentaries that have been written on *Invisible Man* during the past twenty years.

II

The Autobiography of an Ex-Colored Man, like Frederick Douglass's *Narrative of the Life of Frederick Douglass* (1845) and William Wells Brown's *Narrative of William Wells Brown, a Fugitive Slave* (1847), opens with a first-person narrator who belongs to the literary class known (since the days of the abolitionist movement) as the "tragic mulatto." Neither Douglass nor Brown can say with certainty when he was born, and both have heard rumors that their father was a white man. Johnson's narrator has only the vaguest memories of the time and place of his birth, and his father is recalled as the white man who came to his mother's small house several times a week. The setting is the rural South, complete with the white aristocrat and his black mistress. While this certainly fits one turn-of-the-century

[19]

literary perspective, Johnson's narrator handles the situation with a telling irony more characteristic of Douglass or Brown than of the Plantation Tradition. When he decides to marry a white woman, the aristocrat must send his mistress away. This situation has a direct parallel in the relationship between the heroine and her lover in William Wells Brown's *Clotel* (1854), but the invective and polemicism (not to mention the maudlin sentimentality) that surround the departure in Brown's novel are almost totally absent in Johnson's. The narrator's simple and detached description in *The Autobiography of an Ex-Colored Man* offers an astute and ironical commentary on the South:

> I remember distinctly the last time this tall man came to the little house in Georgia; that evening before I went to bed he took me up in his arms and squeezed me very tightly; my mother stood behind his chair wiping tears from her eyes. I remember how I sat upon his knee and watched him laboriously drill a hole through a ten-dollar gold piece, and then tie the coin around my neck with a string. I have worn that gold piece around my neck the greater part of my life, and still possess it, but more than once I have wished that some other way had been found of attaching it to me besides putting a hole through it.[4]

The gold piece is not only worthless but also serves as a symbol of the commercial transactions to which black Americans were prey during the days of American slavery. The skillful mood-building and the undercurrent of criticism that characterize the opening scenes run through the novel; and the narrator maintains his state of clinical detachment to the last.

The narrator and his mother make the journey to the North that was so much a part of America's Reconstruction period, and in Connecticut his musical ability makes its first appearance. He quickly learns to play the piano by listening to his mother's renderings of old Southern songs and is designated by the local newspaper an "infant prodigy." He also has keen reading abilities and absorbs instruction and entertainment from books unknown to his peers. In a sense, the progression of his musical tastes is the reverse of his literary development. In music he moves from the songs of his mother's heritage to the Western classics; while in reading he moves from the Bible through *Uncle Tom's Cabin* and the works of Alexandre Dumas and Frederick Douglass. The protagonist's reading constitutes a type of abolitionist history, since he overcomes the lure of Western Christianity, acquires enlightenment from the work of Harriet Beecher Stowe, resolves to be a race man at a commencement speech on Toussaint L'Ouverture, and ends with the adoption of one of the greatest black abolitionists as his hero. The narrator has been forced toward this moral and intellectual awakening by a classroom incident in which the teacher asked all of the white children to stand up and abruptly told him that he did not belong among them. The event finds its most elucidating parallel in "Of Our Spiritual Strivings," the first chapter of W. E. B. Du Bois's *The Souls of Black Folk*:

> I remember well when the shadow swept across me. I was a little thing, away up in the hills of New England, where the dark Housatonic winds between Hoosac and Taghkanic to the sea. In a wee wooden schoolhouse, something put it into the boys' and girls' heads to buy gorgeous visiting-cards—ten cents a package—and exchange. The exchange was merry, till one girl, a tall newcomer, refused my card—refused it peremptorily, with a glance. Then it dawned upon me with a certain suddenness that I was different from the others; or like, mayhap, in heart and life and longing, but shut out from their world by a vast veil.[5]

Just as Du Bois grows more introspective after his encounter, so Johnson's protagonist retreats into a world of books and music and becomes aware of what Du Bois calls the "double consciousness" that fragments the black self:

> And so I have often lived through that hour, that day, that week, in which was wrought the miracle of my transition from one world into another; for I did indeed pass into another world. . . . And this is the dwarfing, warping, distorting influence which operates upon each and every coloured man in the United States. He is forced to take his outlook on all things, not from the view-point of a citizen, or a man, or even a human being, but from the view-point of a *coloured* man. It is wonderful to me that the race has progressed so broadly as it has, since most of its thought and all of its activity must run through the narrow neck of this one funnel. (P. 403)

Johnson had read and been greatly impressed by Du Bois's work,[6] and it is not surprising that the mulatto status and the varying musical inclinations of his narrator act as symbolic projections of a double consciousness. The narrator modulates between the black world and the white (often with less than equanimity), and seems torn between the early melodies of his mother and the Chopinesque style that wins his white beloved. In a sense, *The Autobiography of an Ex-Colored Man* is a fictional rendering of *The Souls of Black Folk*, for Johnson's narrator stresses not only his bifurcated vision but also his intellectual genius. He maintains an open, critical attitude toward the many sides of black American culture, condemns in unequivocal terms the limitations of the black situation, and assiduously records his movement from a naïve provincialism toward a broad cosmopolitanism. The narrator, in short, is a black man of culture recording the situations and attitudes that have succeeded in driving him underground, to a position the larger society might define as criminal:

> I know that in writing the following pages I am divulging the great secret of my life, the secret which for some years I have guarded far more carefully than any of my earthly possessions; and it is a curious study to me that I am led by the same impulse which forces the un-found-out criminal to take somebody into his confidence, although he knows that the act is likely, even almost certain, to lead to his undoing. (P. 393)

The Autobiography of an Ex-Colored Man is both the history and the confession of one of the "talented tenth" (that class of college-bred black Americans in whom Du Bois placed so much faith); it offers the rehearsal of a "soul on ice" who draws substance from a world that could not recognize his true character or sympathize with his longings. Each of its episodes is an effort at personal definition and a partial summing up of the black American past.

The narrator goes South to attend a black college established by the Freedmen's Bureau and Northern philanthropy; he circulates among the Southern black folk, and discovers (in the manner of Booker T. Washington) the value of a trade for an ambitious black man. He (like the more than two million blacks who left the South between 1890 and 1920) is driven by economic conditions to migrate to the North again, and he chooses to work out his destiny in New York. Quickly throwing off the pursuit of "useful work," he becomes involved in the underworld of black urban life (which had not yet moved uptown to Harlem), and he is one of the earliest recorders of the new black urban condition:

> New York City is the most fatally fascinating thing in America. She sits like a great witch at the gate of the country, showing her alluring white

face and hiding her crooked hands and feet under the folds of her wide
garments—constantly enticing thousands from far within, and tempting
those who come across the seas to go no farther. And all these become the
victims of her caprice. (P. 442)

After such a description, it is not surprising to find the narrator
caught in a dissipating ritual of gambling, late hours, and heady
pleasures. But there is also insight. He describes one aspect of the city
life of his day—the successful black jockeys, the black entertainers
who acted on the minstrel stage, while they possessed the talent of
fine tragedians, the affluent hustlers and the badman heroes who
brought white society slumming. Moreover, it is at this period in
his wanderings that he recognizes the greatness of black musicians, those "unknown bards" who originated ragtime and jazz
and found them copied by white musicians, who made a fortune.
After an encounter with a black badman (in which a wealthy white
woman plays a significant role), the narrator goes to Europe with a
decadent American millionaire who has found release from ennui
in his music. He thus becomes one of the first fictional black artistic exiles (John A. Williams's and Cecil Brown's protagonists in *The
Man Who Cried I Am* and *The Life and Loves of Mr. Jiveass Nigger*
are others of a more recent vintage) to grow expansive in a European setting. Finally, however, the pull of his heritage, his am-
bition to be an influential black American, and an ironic incident
in which he witnesses a European musician turn the raw material
of ragtime into classical harmonies lead him to return to the United
States. Like the Alexander Crummell whom Du Bois portrays in
The Souls of Black Folk, he overcomes the temptation to remain
in exile and refuses to attend his patron's siren song on the intractability of the American racial problem.

The last quarter of *The Autobiography of an Ex-Colored Man*
concerns the narrator's attempt to become a transcriber of cultural
values; like the speaker in Jean Toomer's "Song of the Son," he
returns to the South to gather the seeds of his heritage in order to
transform them into "An everlasting song, a singing tree,/Caroling
softly souls of slavery,/What they were, and what they are to me,/
Caroling softly souls of slavery."[7] He sets out to collect the folk

songs of his mother's people and to transcribe them into the written, Western forms that will preserve them and insure their recognition. There is an implicit optimism at this point in the novel, since the narrator is now an educated and traveled man (having made the "grand tour" and acquired one or two foreign languages) who seems capable of realizing his early ambitions; he has come full circle, returning to the land of his birth dedicated to an enterprise that will raise its "forgotten man" from a position that was occupied by his own mother. Unlike Du Bois, however, who could call for the recognition of *The Souls of Black Folk* in his "After-Thought," the narrator never has the opportunity to complete his task. The chattel principle (a fundamental assumption of the American slave system) drives him from the South. The principle—which asserts that blacks are property to be worked, whipped, and herded about at will—was reinforced by the Dred Scott decision (1857) handed down by Chief Justice Roger B. Taney and the Supreme Court itself, and the informing force of *The Autobiography of an Ex-Colored Man* derives from its presence as the *sine qua non* in black-white relationships in America.[8] The protagonist witnesses the burning alive of a black man and is overcome with humiliation that he is a member of a group that the country at large considers beneath the status of animals. He comments:

> All the while I understood that it was not discouragement or fear or search for a larger field of action and opportunity that was driving me out of the Negro race. I knew that it was shame, unbearable shame. Shame at being identified with a people that could with impunity be treated worse than animals. For certainly the law would restrain and punish the malicious burning alive of animals. (P. 499)

His reaction is as bitter and telling as the reflections of his early hero—Frederick Douglass—on the same situation: "They [professing Christians who own slaves and support slavery] would be shocked at the proposition of fellowshipping a *sheep*-stealer; and at the same time they hug to their communion a *man*-stealer, and brand me with being an infidel, if I find fault with them for it."[9]

The Autobiography of an Ex-Colored Man, in its treatment of the chattel principle, moves toward the category of the protest novel, and its denunciation of Southern inhumanity is particularly effective since the lynching scene climaxes the novel and brings to an end the narrator's hopes for the art of his people. The process of culture-building and broad humanistic development comes to an abrupt halt as the narrator is forced to take the lesser course: he joins the vast white American fraternity that considers money-making the acme of human virtue. It is not surprising, therefore, that the novel concludes with stock situations: the tragic mulatto passing for white and chuckling at the great joke he is playing on society; his sudden depression (with shades of Charles Chesnutt's *The House Behind the Cedars* and William Dean Howells's *An Imperative Duty*) when he falls in love with a white woman; *amor vincit omnia* as the white, blond, and blue-eyed ideal accepts his proposal; and the resultant happiness of brighter mulattoes and more money in the family. Yet the overall tragic dimensions of the narrative are heightened by the protagonist's realization that he has sold his birthright for what might be (and his employment of hackneyed literary conventions supports his suspicions) "a mess of pottage." He has rendered his confession as a lesson to those who will follow, and his story—which celebrates black folk culture and depicts the tragic dilemma of the black situation—concludes with the narrator in a somewhat static condition of endless self-recrimination. In his role as an artist—an individual who sees, evaluates, and records— however, there resides an influential and seminal dynamism.

III

The cultural situation that produced *The Autobiography of an Ex-Colored Man*, the manner in which the story is set forth, and the antecedent works that influenced its author lead one easily to the informing sensibility and significant patterns of action in *Invisible Man*. *Invisible Man* begins with the same situation that opens the *Narrative of the Life of Frederick Douglass* and *The Autobiography of an Ex-Colored Man*; the narrator is writing a retrospective account of his life from a position of impunity (his warm hole in a basement). Like the fugitive Douglass, who risked capture by writing his story, and the "passing" narrator of Johnson's novel, he is outside the white laws of the land, for he is covertly drawing substance from the white world above and has assaulted one of its inhabitants. These similarities are heightened by the presence of black American slav-

[25]

ery at the opening of *Invisible Man*. The fantasy that comes to the narrator when he has unwittingly smoked a reefer while listening to Louis Armstrong's "What Did I Do to Be so Black and Blue" contains the auction block, the miscegenation of the master class ("a beautiful girl the color of ivory"), the ironical subversion of the blacks themselves ("I loved him and give him the poison and he withered away like a frost-bit apple"), and the old-time black American preacher. Johnson's narrator, since his work begins "a few years after the close of the Civil War," uses the slave past and surrounds it with several literary conventions that were popular in the Plantation Tradition; Ellison's narrator, on the other hand, purports to back away from this past, stating that "hearing around corners" is unbearable. In reality, the invisible man is just as concerned with the origins of his culture as the ex-colored man, and the brief view presented in the Prologue must be grasped if one is to fully understand *Invisible Man*.

The issue is the definition of freedom, and the antagonists are: first, the narrator's unwillingness to look beneath the surface of things; and, second, those members of his race who act as agencies for a brutal white world. He backs away from the old woman who talks of liberation and is pursued down a dark tunnel by her sons, mulatto victims of a miscegenatory South. Of course, a number of Freudian and symbolistic interpretations are possible here, but the essential fact seems to be that the narrator has begun the process of "running" toward freedom and identity, which resembles the action of William Craft's narrator in *Running a Thousand Miles for Freedom* (1860), that eventually lands him underground and forces him to the artistry of his narrative. Chapter One ("The Battle Royal") elucidates this initial situation; it shows the invisible man, like the ex-colored man, exploring the possibilities of the American South and discovering many of the same aspects that appear in *The Autobiography of an Ex-Colored Man*: class division, duplicity, and the chattel principle. The chapter not only enlarges the compressed view of slavery presented in the Prologue, but also illuminates the remaining episodes in the novel. From the outset the narrator has been co-opted by the white world; he has been chosen to replace one of the scheduled fighters in the battle royal, and this sets the other participants against him. The episode flows outward from this act of white insensitivity—or cunning, as the case may be. The boys are tempted by a white stripteaser with an American flag tattooed on her stomach (the American white female, a lauded symbol of virtue, who must be protected at all costs) before they are blindfolded and pitted against one another in a boxing ring, where the victor (an ironical designation here) is to be the last one standing. There is not only intraracial violence (like that of the mulattoes against the narrator in the Prologue) but also intraracial conspiracy, since the smaller fighters have agreed to slip out of the ring and leave the narrator alone with Tatlock, "the biggest of the gang," who knocks him out. When the blindfolds are removed, the boys are forced to scamper after coins on an electrified rug, and only at the last is the narrator—having suffered at the hands of perverse Southern white men, and swallowing his own blood—allowed to make his Booker T. Washingtonian speech urging blacks to cultivate friendly relations with whites and search for opportunity in the South. The hostility that rises from the audience when he mistakenly says "social equality" instead of "social responsibility" and the briefcase containing a scholarship to an accommodationist black college are his rewards, and they further define his hearers.

\ The invisible man's briefcase serves the same function as the ten-dollar gold piece in *The Autobiography of an Ex-Colored Man*; the nature of the American situation makes it a worthless item that plagues the narrator for the remainder of the novel. The images and themes of the battle royal scene in toto share this treadmill effect; most of them recur in slightly altered forms throughout the narration. The intraracial violence is repeated in the Liberty Paints episode (the struggle between Brockway and the protagonist), in the Men's House episode, in the scene that pits Ras the Destroyer against Clifton and the invisible man, and in the concluding riot. The white stripteaser finds her counterparts in Emma, in the white woman who seduces the narrator after a Brotherhood lecture, and in the directionless Sybil. The electric carpet (perhaps symbolic of the awesome mechanistic and technological power of the white world) finds its parallels in the machinery of Liberty Paints and in the lobotomizing machine in the factory hospital. The narrator's oratory—which compares

[27]

favorably with the musical ability of the ex-colored man—comes to
the forefront again in the dispossession episode, the Brotherhood
episode, and Tod Clifton's funeral. Images of blindness and vision
are too numerous to mention,[10] and the battle royal scene as a whole
is recalled when the narrator prepares to make his first speech for the
Brotherhood. The setting is a boxing arena, and before he goes into
the ring to speak, he notices a poster of a black fighter who was
blinded in a corrupt contest.

Invisible Man is surely a rich and complex work of art, but it
does not seem far from the mark to say the battle royal episode constitutes its most significant projection and fully justifies its comparison with The Autobiography of an Ex-Colored Man. The narrators of
both works undergo many restless turnings within what appears to
be a circular pattern (with the end in the beginning), each repeatedly
colliding with the indisputable facts of the American situation—its
denial of the black man and its avid willingness to co-opt and exploit
his talents. In The Autobiography of an Ex-Colored Man, both the
narrator (by his millionaire patron) and his mother (by her aristo-
cratic lover) are treated like pawns to relieve the ennui or further the
designs of the white world, and in Invisible Man the narrator is
ricocheted from one brutal and dehumanizing episode to the next by a
society bent on securing ideological and materialistic advantages.
Ellison's narrator does not make as many physical journeys as Johnson's, but his emblematic and imaginative scenes carry the reader
over much of the same ground. The dispossession scene, for example,
with its knocking bones, potted plants, and free papers, calls up
the entire black agrarian heritage; the sambo bank (which reads
"Feed Me") that the narrator breaks as he demands civilized behavior
from the residents of a Harlem tenement is equivalent to Johnson's
long expositions on the "desperate class" of black America; the sermon that confronts the narrator in his fantasy, and his description of
the singing at Clifton's funeral are equivalent to Johnson's treatment
of "Big Meeting" in Alabama. What impresses one most in comparing the two works, however, is their similarity on the deeper, ex-
periential plane of thought and emotion.

On this plane, the substantive issue is freedom for the black
man in America, and the narrators of both The Autobiography of an

Ex-Colored Man and *Invisible Man* seem to realize that the products and achievements of the folk cannot be minimized in reaching this goal. Both works read, at times, like folk histories,[11] since they treat the major stages of the black man's experience in America: slavery, the South, miscegenation (the invisible man, not incidentally, is "ginger colored"), the black college experience, the migration to the North, and contact with capitalism and philanthropy. Of course, *Invisible Man*, coming at a later date, extends this panorama to include industrialism, trade unionism, communism, and black nationalism. Both narrators pay tribute to the folk themselves by chronicling their artistry and allowing their values to inform their respective stories: the values of the trickster in the invisible man's grandfather; the badman hero of Johnson's New York and the daring Tarp of the Brotherhood; a southern boarding house, where communal ideals and soulful cooking are in the forefront, and Mary Rambo's in Harlem; the attitudes of black sermons and spirituals in Johnson's Alabama and Ellison's New York, and the decisive position the posture of Frederick Douglass holds in both novels. Finally, there is Ellison's unforgettable Trueblood. The name alone of this black storyteller (who lives in an "enduring" Southern slave cabin) indicates his authenticity as a folk projection, and the entire episode constitutes a brief drama of slavery. Mr. Norton, the white voyeur, pays the black raconteur for his entrancing tale. Trueblood, meanwhile, takes the role of folk poet— but also that of the black breeder. During the days of American slavery the production of ten children for the master's stores sometimes secured a slave's manumission, and in a world where the phrase "black family" was often a misnomer, the Western horror of incest must have been minimized. While Norton grows faint and sightless at "the horror, the horror" (to use Conrad's words from a similar situation), Trueblood has a firm grasp of the situation. He overcomes his angst and suffering by that "near-tragic, near-comic lyricism" which Ellison has described as characteristic of the blues.[12] He secures, moreover, a handsome profit and a measure of freedom by means of his broad folk wisdom.

Informing both *The Autobiography of an Ex-Colored Man* and *Invisible Man* are the cultured stance and carefully delineated "double consciousness" found in W. E. B. Du Bois's *The Souls of Black Folk*. Both the invisible man and the ex-colored man are concerned with their relationship to what Du Bois calls "the problem of the Twentieth Century . . . the color line"; each modulates between an exclusive dedication to black American culture and an attempt to secure the privilege, acclaim, and freedom from (again in Du Bois's words) "the other world which does not know and does not want to know our power." The paradox here is that the narrators' accomplished designs and carefully stated black themes make both *The Autobiography of an Ex-Colored Man* and *Invisible Man* resolutions of the alternatives. Both works have gained plaudits from the larger American community, and both have secured freedom and privilege for the black American writer, who finds both an object lesson in his craft and the singular achievements of his culture rendered by the novels. And the dedication of *The Autobiography of an Ex-Colored Man* and *Invisible Man* to the spirit of black American culture and the liberation of its citizens abides the questions of both militant ideologues and adherents to the codes of a highly structuralist criticism.

IV

As a final word, one might say that the best justification for comparing the works of James Weldon Johnson and Ralph Ellison is to be found in the criticism that has been devoted to proving *Invisible Man* a prime example of twentieth-century symbolism or *The Autobiography of an Ex-Colored Man* a latter-day picaresque without treating the singularly black American character of either novel. This, of course, is not a call for that time-honored formula—"the Negro novel"—nor is it meant as a blanket condemnation of efforts such as those mentioned above. Yet when one realizes that *Invisible Man* is part of an accomplished tradition that extends from Briton Hammon through Frederick Douglass, James Weldon Johnson, Langston Hughes, and Richard Wright—a tradition predicated upon a complex folk heritage and informed in the twentieth century by the work of W. E. B. Du Bois—one must protest a statement such as the following:

Technically *Invisible Man* is a *tour de force*, using a whole spectrum of fictional techniques to convey a complex authorial attitude and build a fictional world which transcends realistic description or simple probability. The action shifts from nitty-gritty realism to hallucinatory fantasy without a break in the seams of style. It is a virtuoso performance, moving from unsophisticated methods to highly complex and subtle modes of narration. . . .[13]

The comparative method—with all of its pitfalls—seems far preferable to this type of flamboyant, structuralist word play. It helps to elucidate the "existing monuments" that lead to *Invisible Man*, and it offers keys to an understanding of such recent works as *The Autobiography of Malcolm X*, George Cain's *Blueschild Baby*, and Barry Beckham's *My Main Mother*.

IV

Paul Laurence Dunbar, an Evaluation

He came, a dark youth, singing in the dawn
Of a new freedom, glowing o'er his lyre,
Refining, as with great Apollo's fire,
His people's gift of song. . . .
—JAMES D. CORROTHERS

WITH Paul Laurence Dunbar, we enter a new world of black artistry, for Dunbar was surely the first black American to make a career of belles lettres. "The first black American poet of distinction" is the title normally accorded Dunbar, and for years friends, fellow black men, and detractors have had their go at his reputation. Their chief concern is the poet's place in literature, his rank as an artist. In his day Dunbar was acknowledged, lauded, and feted by the greatest—Frederick Douglass (at the Chicago Exposition, in 1893), Booker T. Washington (on several occasions), John Hay (while in England), Theodore Roosevelt (at various times). William Dean Howells, one of the foremost critics in turn-of-the-century America, called him "the first poet of his race."[1] Howells's championing of the poet's cause did little harm, for after his puff in *Harper's Weekly*, Dunbar's poems, short stories, novels, and public readings were well received and patronized. And while whites patronized, most blacks looked on with pride—here was a black man who had achieved success as an American writer. The novelty of his situation is captured by Victor Lawson:

> . . . he was a blazer of trails, both in journalism and in the direction of *belles lettres*. Negroes had not ventured much into the world of writing on a professional level until Dunbar's time. He showed them the way, almost alone, against great odds of prejudice, poverty, and ill health.[2]

A black American blazing trails "against great odds"—the picture is a stirring one, and it has called forth accounts that ring true in a number of respects. The stacked odds began with Joshua and Matilda Dunbar, the poet's parents, both former slaves. With a heritage commencing in slavery, Dunbar finished high school and started to work as an elevator operator for a salary of four dollars a week; it was while he held this job that *Oak and Ivy* (1893), his first volume of verse, was published. Throughout his life the poet's state failed to rise far above these inauspicious beginnings. He had an unhappy marriage, which terminated in separation and pain; he was a victim of tuberculosis, and the "dark angel" of alcoholism haunted him always. From the barest biography, therefore, we can recognize the justice of accounts that portray Dunbar struggling against great odds.

Integrally involved with the biographical facts, moreover, are certain socio-historical and psychological facts that reinforce the picture of the struggling artist. On the socio-historical plane the facts are the same as those one views in the case of Booker T. Washington. Dunbar's first acknowledged volume of verse, *Lyrics of Lowly Life*, was published (with an introduction by Howells) in 1896; his death came in 1906. The intervening ten years marked part of the most brutal, oppressive, and imperialistic era in American history; this was the age of "Jim Crow," "the Klan," and "the white man's burden"; the words "colored" and "evil" were deemed synonymous, and the synonymity was sanctioned by the laws of the land. Just as the education that Booker T. Washington recommended for black Americans at the turn of the century had to be of a very special type, so the literature of the black American had to be of a very special type if it was to be approved by white America. And here we come to the psychological factors.

[34]

Washington had to search conscience and soul before he could set forth his philosophy of education, but since his orientation was basically individualistic and capitalistic, he did not seem to experience great difficulty gliding into harmony with his age. Matters are different, however, with Dunbar—the sensitive, talented black man who wanted more than anything to create beauty. His problem has been justly labeled by Saunders Redding as one of "cultural" and "psychological dualism."[3] Just as he was set apart from the cultural mainstream by whites, so he was torn internally by the question of writing honestly and not being read or accepted by white audiences, or writing falsely and being read and accepted. In a sense Dunbar's choice was between success and failure. Washington chose success and built Tuskegee into a thriving institution lauded by America; Dunbar also decided on success and wrote poems lauded by America. The different attitudes of the general public toward the spheres of endeavor of the two men, however, make the success of the capitalist a more permanent thing (since property and profit are always topics of admiration) than the temporal success of the artist. (Who, for example, reads Martin Tupper today?) Perhaps the differentiation between the two men can be stated in temporal terms; Washington was a man of his times, a man of industry who accepted the American myths of self-help, free competition, and useful work. Dunbar, on the other hand, was a black Miniver Cheevy; his artistic gaze was turned to the past, and the myths that he adopted were already under scrutiny and attack when *Lyrics of Love and Laughter* appeared in the same year (1903) as *The Souls of Black Folk*. Washington set forth an individualistic, industrial perspective that finds its counterpart in today's black capitalism, coalition venture corporations, and urban coalitions; Dunbar, on the other hand, set forth an antebellum perspective that finds its sternest opponents among today's black Americans.

A critical ambivalence thus surrounds the name, work, and reputation of Paul Laurence Dunbar. On one hand we have the struggling, oppressed black artist who blazed a trail for his race; on the other, we have the culturally and psychologically torn black man who adopted outmoded myths and achieved a limited success. The innumerable factors that produce this irresolution cannot be shifted into neat categories; if they could be, there would be no irresolution. Nonetheless, there are certain considerations—beyond the socio-historical one and its attendant psychological distortions—that are relevant to our evaluation of Dunbar.

The first consideration is the artistic milieu in which the poet worked, and here we can paraphrase T. S. Eliot's comments on William Blake:[4] the fault is perhaps not with Dunbar himself but with the environment that failed to provide what such a poet needed. Dunbar was a man interested in the conscious creation of works of literature out of the experiences that were closest to hand, those of his own life, the life of a black man in America. And just as Blake (according to Eliot) could find no clear and formulated perspective in the intellectual fabric of his age, so Dunbar could find no honest and carefully articulated picture of the experiences that he found most suited to his artistic purposes. It was not so much that he "required" and "sadly lacked . . . a framework of accepted and traditional ideas which would have prevented him from engaging in a philosophy of his own . . ."; the fact is that the framework was so present and distorted that only an incredibly strong man could have embraced a philosophy of his own. The type of strength that Dunbar needed is usually found at the high points of a continuous literary tradition rather than at the outset; and so we are left with the poet facing an omnipresent and distorted framework.

It was, in part, an enervated romanticism that gave forth the femme fatale, Byronic poses, exotic images, melancholia, and gentle and maidenly idylls in pastoral settings (which never were on land or sea) that constituted the framework in which Dunbar wrote. Lawson has traced the origins of this framework to the great English Romantic poets and sees its gradual diminution as it passes from Tennyson and Browning to the American Romantics—Bryant and Poe. The most undernourished verses are those that came from Dunbar's immediate predecessors. Here is Bryant:

. . . When thoughts
Of the last bitter hour come like a blight
. . . .
Go forth under the open sky, and list
To nature's teachings . . .
. . . .
 . . . the complaining brooks
That make the meadows green; and, poured 'round all

[36]

Old Ocean's gray and melancholy waste—
Are but the solemn decorations all
Of the great tomb of man! . . .

And here is Bayard Taylor on the "mysterious East": "Daughter of Egypt, veil thine eyes!/I cannot bear their fire . . ." ("A Pledge to Hafiz"). Finally, here is the "breast-forward," optimistic Longfellow:

Let us then, be up and doing
With a heart for any fate;
Still achieving, still pursuing,
Learn to labor and to wait.
                    ("A Psalm of Life")

Number along with these Edward Coate Pinkney ("Look out upon the stars, my love,/ And shame them with thine eyes,/ On which, than on the lights above,/ There hang more destinies") and Henry Timrod ("Sleep sweetly in your humble graves,/ Sleep, martyrs of a fallen cause;/ Though yet no marble column craves/ The pilgrim here to pause"). Consider John Greenleaf Whittier's "Snow-Bound," Oliver Wendell Holmes's "The Living Temple," most of the work of Richard Stoddard, Thomas Aldrich, Edmund Stedman, Eugene Field, Richard Hovey, and James Whitcomb Riley, and you have part of the framework that Dunbar looked to. Of course, you would be justified if you said it was not very inspiring for a young artist— these romantic echoes bouncing off American walls.

But so far we have seen only *part* of the framework; this has been merely the large, general picture—unillumined, of course, by Walt Whitman and Emily Dickinson. The other part is even less inspiring, and one is not to be blamed or castigated if the names here do not ring a familiar tone—they are best forgotten. Here we have Stephen Collins Foster writing of "The Old Folks at Home," and J. A. Macon on Uncle Gabe Tucker and his people; we see Joel Chandler Harris's simple child of nature, Uncle Remus, and view the obsequious, laughable, obedient, and queer black folks of Frank Stanton, Thomas Nelson Page, and Irwin Russell. Such lyricists and narrators were bent on producing works that showed a bright and glorious antebellum South, the Plantation Tradition in all its glory. And their method comprised an unskilled use of black American dialect, a

[37]

host of stereotyped characters, and all the myths of black inferiority one could muster. It wasn't new: T. D. Rice started it when he stole a dance from a black slave and carried it to the stage with his face appropriately blacked. The Fosters, Harrises, and Russells are simply the culmination of the minstrel tradition in America, and their work presents a fairly accurate picture of the view America held of the black man during the late-nineteenth and early-twentieth centuries. But this was the accepted picture of the experiences that Dunbar found suited to his artistic purposes. Does it not seem fair to say the picture was neither honest nor "carefully articulated"? Sterling Brown notes the distortions of character and needless misspellings of the whole school of black dialect poets,[5] and one hastens to add that black American poets such as James Campbell (whom Dunbar knew and possibly emulated), Daniel Webster Davis, and J. Mord Allen shared most of the faults of Macon, Stanton, and other white writers.

To bring things into focus at this point is to perceive a less-than-brilliant prospect for the late-nineteenth-century poet, whether black or white. The faded romanticism of pastoral and jingoistic poets combined with the mawkish, misspelled sentimentalism of antebellum aggrandizers—the combination can hardly be called a stable framework for the aspiring poet; and if the poet happened to be black, he saw his aspirations mocked in the very framework he was expected to employ. On the literary plane, therefore, on the plane that Eliot called "traditional," we can see Dunbar burdened by weights as heavy as those on the socio-historical and psychosocial levels.

And the introduction of American realism and naturalism scarcely brightens the prospect. It is true that writers like Howells, Hamlin Garland, Stephen Crane, Frank Norris, and Theodore Dreiser had made their respective and notable appearances on the literary scene; the first three, in fact, had received considerable plaudits. Howells was hindered in his appreciation of the younger writers, however, by his belief that beneath the surface difficulties life always wears a smiling face ("Morality penetrates all things"). The new group of writers was bent on probing the less sanguine aspects of life, on going to the depths of society and the individual psyche. Even Mark Twain realized by the 1890s that he and Howells were like "two old derelicts." But if realism found itself *démodé*, was naturalism any more fashionable in its early days? *Main-Travelled Roads* (1891), *The Red Badge of Courage* (1895), and selected works of Norris were celebrated to be sure, but Dreiser's *Sister Carrie,* published in 1900, was suppressed until 1912. Moreover, the grim and cynical picture of life in the verse of Edwin Arlington Robinson had to wait two decades for recognition. More important to the present discussion is the fact that both Garland and Crane turned to romances (a potboiler in the case of Crane) before their careers were ended. The popular taste demanded sentimental romance and historical adventure; the mass-circulation magazines supplied both. A consideration of realism and naturalism, therefore, does little to alter the description of the framework in which Dunbar labored.

Our critical ambivalence veers in favor of the poet. At this point, however, we must recall Wilde's dictum that great art is always in advance of its age, and common sense and our own literary awareness tell us that great individuals always transcend the group that provides their maturing and value. In short, the literary master, the genius, is never of a particular epoch, and with this in mind, one might acknowledge that Dunbar was neither a literary master nor a man of genius. The counterbalancing factors—a militantly rebellious spirit and a keen perception of the conditions of artistic greatness along with a Keatsian desire to achieve it—which might have lifted the poet above his age were absent in the life of Dunbar. Hence, the first black American poet of distinction remains an artist rooted in time and incomprehensible without a thorough understanding of the age that provided the symbols for his art.

This is not to say that Dunbar lacks importance for us; while a glance from the age to the poet and back gives us (in part) a mirror image, it can give more. First, the implications of the image speak of a certain greatness; in Dunbar's work we find the black American's peril-filled struggle to literacy blossoming into accomplished (though at times facile, at times false) verse. For a black American to equal his poetic contemporaries, given the history of black America, was no mean achievement; for him to achieve skill and fame in "Jim Crow" America was an overwhelming one. Behind the image, in short, is the story of a successful struggle against literary, socio-historical and psychological odds. The story is inseparable from the artistic corpus, and together they give to humanity—and to struggling black humanity in particular—a thing of value.

Second, Dunbar's canon, in some of the more skilled efforts, represents an artistic merger of the highest importance for both the black and the white American literary traditions. The conscious literary craftsmanship of black orator, romantic, and formalist poets combines with the essence of the black American folk tradition in his canon with results that are often striking. Dunbar grew up in a home where stories of the "old days" in slavery were frequent, and his early formal education by his mother was spiced with folk anecdotes. In a town like Dayton, Ohio, where the black population was small and Dunbar the only black student in his high school class, opportunities for communicating with the folk must have been limited. But the poet worked in hotels, as a waiter, and as an elevator operator during his career, and these occupations put him in contact with some of the more fundamental rhythms of his culture. Like Harriet Beecher Stowe, he also profited from living in the border state of Ohio; neighboring Kentucky provided stories, individuals, and traditions growing out of slavery. And one suspects that a number of his writings—like "The Haunted Oak" and "The Ingrate," a biographical effort detailing Joshua Dunbar's escape from bondage—had their inception in stories told to him by black men who had seen slavery firsthand. In 1899, Dunbar himself traveled to the deep South to give a series of readings. The oral folk tradition was, thus, important to the poet's development; his travels, voracious reading, and, most of all, his poverty, gave him a sense of the folk.

The vitality, humor, communality, protest, acuity, idiom, and fused strength that characterized the southern, agrarian black folk find expression in a number of poems that are incredible for their melodiousness and finish. "Philosophy," "An Ante-Bellum Sermon," "The Party," and "When Malindy Sings" are but four of the poems in which Dunbar captures the best of both worlds; he is the accomplished American writer, and he is an honest spokesman for the folk. The results may appear simple, but that is one of the traits of fine art—a seeming ease of composition. In actuality, the skilled blending of southern folk regionalism with a conscious literary tradition has reached high points only in the work of some of the most notable

American authors—Langston Hughes, Jean Toomer, Sterling Brown, Erskine Caldwell, and William Faulkner. Thus Dunbar points, on occasion, to the classics of the twentieth century, and the merger of the folk and the conscious literary traditions that he brought about has proved one of the most important facets of black American literature from his day to the present.

We are left with a portrait of an artist who gave to humanity a gift of example: a paradigm of the creative spirit overcoming mammoth odds. And at times Dunbar's verse breaks from the confines of a narrow and distorted framework. The better poems serve as correctives to the flaccid romanticism and false antebellum sentimentalism that infused the age in which they were written. They provide a true picture of a strong and enduring people and point directions for some of the finest literary works of this century. Dunbar's gifts were of value, and with just recognition they must prove permanent.

V

The Achievement of Gwendolyn Brooks

A writer writes out of his own family background, out of his own immediate community, during his formative period. And he writes out of his
own talent and his own individual vision. Now if he doesn't, if he tries
to get away from that by bending it to some ideological line, then he is
depriving the group of its uniqueness. What we need is individuals. If
the white society has tried to do anything to us, it has tried to keep us
from being individuals.

—RALPH ELLISON

WENDOLYN Brooks, like W. E. B. Du Bois, seems
caught between two worlds. And both she and Du Bois manifest the
duality of their lives in their literary works; Du Bois wrote in a
beautiful, impressionistic style set off by quotations from the
world's literary masters. Miss Brooks writes tense, complex,
rhythmic verse that contains the metaphysical complexities of John
Donne and the word magic of Appollinaire, Eliot, and Pound. The
high style of both authors, however, is often used to explicate the
condition of the black American trapped behind a veil that
separates him from the white world. What one seems to have is
"white" style and "black" content—two warring ideals in one dark
body.

[43]

This apparent dichotomy has produced a confusing situation for Gwendolyn Brooks. The world of white arts and letters has pointed to her with pride; it has bestowed kudos and a Pulitzer Prize. The world of black arts and letters has looked on with mixed emotion, and pride has been only one part of the mixture. There have also been troubling questions about the poet's essential "blackness," her dedication to the melioration of the black American's social conditions. The real duality appears when we realize that Gwendolyn Brooks—though praised and awarded—does not appear on the syllabi of most American literature courses, and her name seldom appears in the annual scholarly bibliographies of the academic world. It would seem she is a black writer after all, *not* an American writer. Yet when one listens to the voice of today's black-revolutionary consciousness, one often hears that Miss Brooks's early poetry fits the white, middle-class patterns Imamu Baraka has seen as characteristic of "Negro literature."[1]

When one turns to her canon, one finds she has abided the questions of both camps. Etheridge Knight has perfectly captured her enduring quality in the following lines:

O courier on Pegasus. O Daughter of Parnassus
O Splendid woman of the purple stitch.
When beaten and blue, despairingly we sink
Within obfuscating mire,
O, cradle in your bosom us, hum your lullabies
And soothe our souls with kisses of verse
That stir us on to search for light.

O Mother of the world. Effulgent lover of the Sun!
For ever speak the truth.[2]

She has the Parnassian inspiration and the earth-mother characteristics noted by the poet; her strength has come from a dedication to truth. The truth that concerns her does not amount to a facile realism or a heavy naturalism, though "realism" is the word that comes to mind when one reads a number of poems in *A Street in Bronzeville* (1945).

Poems, or segments, such as "kitchenette building," "a song in the front yard," and "the vacant lot," all support the view that the

[44]

writer was intent on a realistic, even a naturalistic, portrayal of the life of lower-echelon urban dwellers:

We are things of dry hours and the involuntary plan,
Grayed in, and gray. "Dream" makes a giddy sound, not
    strong
Like "rent," "feeding a wife," "satisfying a man."

("kitchenette building")[3]

My mother, she tells me that Johnnie Mae
Will grow up to be a bad woman.
That George'll be taken to Jail soon or late
(On account of last winter he sold our back gate.)

("a song in the front yard")

And with seeing the squat fat daughter
Letting in the men
When majesty has gone for the day—
And letting them out again.

("the vacant lot")

These passages reinforce the designation of Miss Brooks as a realist, and poems such as "The Sundays of Satin-Legs Smith," "We Real Cool," "A Lovely Love," and the volume *Annie Allen* can be added to the list. If she had insisted on a strict realism and nothing more, she could perhaps be written off as a limited poet. But she is no mere chronicler of the condition of the black American poor. Even her most vividly descriptive verses contain an element that removes them from the realm of a cramped realism. All of her characters have both ratiocinative and imaginative capabilities; they have the ability to reason, dream, muse, and remember. This ability distinguishes them from the naturalistic literary victim caught in an environmental maze. From the realm of "raw and unadorned life," Satin-Legs Smith creates his own world of bright colors, splendid attire, and soft loves in the midst of a cheap hotel's odor and decay. The heroine of "The Anniad" conjures up a dream world, covers it in silver plate, populates it with an imaginary prince, and shores up magnificent fragments against the ruins of war. And Jessie Mitchell's mother seeks refuge from envy and death in a golden past:

[45]

She revived for the moment settled and dried-up triumphs,
Forced perfume into old petals, pulled up the droop,
Refueled
Trimphant long-exhaled breaths.
Her exquisite yellow youth . . . .

Gwendolyn Brooks's characters, in short, are infinitely human because at the core of their existence is the imaginative intellect.

Given the vision of such characters, it is impossible to agree with
David Littlejohn, who wishes to view them as simplistic mouth-
pieces for the poet's sensibility;[4] moreover, it is not surprising that
the characters' concerns transcend the ghetto life of many black
Americans. They reflect the joy of childhood, the burdens and contentment of motherhood, the distortions of the war-torn psyche, the
horror of blood-guiltiness, and the pains of the anti-hero confronted with a heroic ideal. Miss Brooks's protagonists, personae,
and speakers, in short, capture all of life's complexities and particularly the complexity of an industrialized age characterized by
swift change, depersonalization, and war.

In "Gay Chaps at the Bar," the poet shows her concern for a
theme that has had a great influence on twentieth-century British and
American art. In one section, "my dreams, my works, must wait till
after hell," she employs the food metaphors characteristic of her
writing to express the incompleteness that accompanies war:

I hold my honey and I store my bread
In little jars and cabinets of my will.
I label clearly, and each latch and lid
I bid, Be firm till I return from hell.
I am very hungry. I am incomplete.

In another section, "piano after war," she captures the mental anguish
occasioned by war. The rejuvenation the speaker has felt in the
"golden rose" music feeding his "old hungers" suddenly ends:

But suddenly, across my climbing fever
Of proud delight—a multiplying cry.
A cry of bitter dead men who will never
Attend a gentle maker of musical joy.
Then my thawed eye will go again to ice.
And stone will shove the softness from my face.

In "The Anniad" and the "Appendix to the Anniad," the poet deals

[46]

once again with the chaos of arms: war destroys marriage, stifles fertility, and turns men to creatures of "untranslatable ice." Her work, therefore, joins the mainstream of twentieth-century poetry in its treatment of the terrors of war, and her message comes to us through, as I have mentioned, the imaginative intellect of characters who evoke sympathy and identification.

War, however, is not the only theme that allies Gwendolyn Brooks with the mainstream. One finds telling and ironical speculation in "the preacher: ruminates behind the sermon":

Perhaps—who knows?—He tires of looking down.
Those eyes are never lifted. Never straight.
Perhaps sometimes He tires of being great
In solitude. Without a hand to hold.

In "Strong Men, Riding Horses," we have a Prufrockian portrait of the anti-hero. After his confrontation with the ideals of a Western film, the persona comments:

I am not like that. I pay rent, am addled
By illegible landlords, run, if robbers call.

What mannerisms I present, employ,
Are camouflage, and what my mouths remark
To word-wall off that broadness of the dark
Is pitiful.
I am not brave at all.

In "Mrs. Small," one has a picture of the "Mr. Zeros" (or Willie Lomans) of a complex century, and in "A Bronzeville Mother Loiters in Mississippi. Meanwhile a Mississippi Mother Burns Bacon," we have an evocation of the blood-guiltiness of the white psyche in an age of dying colonialism. Miss Brooks presents these themes with skill because she has the ability to endow each figure with a unique, individualizing vision of the world.

If they were considered in isolation, however, the characters and concerns of the verse would not mark the poet as an outstanding writer. Great poetry demands word magic, a sense of the infinite possibilities of language. In this technical realm Miss Brooks is superb. Her ability to dislocate and mold language into complex patterns of meaning can be observed in her earliest poems and in her

[47]

latest volumes—*In The Mecca* (1968), *Riot* (1969), and *Family Pictures* (1970). The first lines of "The Sundays of Satin-Legs Smith" are illustrative:

INAMORATAS, with an approbation,
Bestowed his title. Blessed his inclination,

He wakes, unwinds, elaborately: a cat
Tawny, reluctant, royal. He is fat
And fine this morning. Definite. Reimbursed.

The handling of polysyllabics is not in the least strained, and the movement is so graceful that one scarcely notices the rhymed couplets. Time and again this word magic is at work, and the poet's varying rhyme schemes lend a subtle resonance that is not found in the same abundance in the works of other acknowledged American writers. It is important to qualify this judgment, however, for while Miss Brooks employs polysyllabics and forces words into striking combinations, she preserves colloquial rhythms. Repeatedly one is confronted by a realistic voice—not unlike that in Robert Frost's poetry—that carries one along the dim corridors of the human psyche or down the rancid halls of a decaying tenement. Miss Brooks's colloquial narrative voice, however, is more prone to complex juxtapositions than Frost's, as a stanza from "The Anniad" illustrates:

Doomer, though, crescendo-comes
Prophesying hecatombs.
Surrealist and cynical.
Garrulous and guttural.
Spits upon the silver leaves.
Denigrates the dainty eves
Dear dexterity achieves.

This surely differs from Frost's stanzas, and the difference resides in the poet's obvious joy in words. She fuses the most elaborate words into contexts that allow them to speak naturally or to sing beautifully her meaning.

Miss Brooks is not indebted to Frost alone for technical influences; she also acknowledges her admiration for Langston Hughes. Though a number of her themes and techniques set her work in the twentieth-century mainstream, there are those that place it firmly in the black American literary tradition. One of her most effective techniques is a sharp, black, comic irony that is closely akin to the scorn Hughes directed at the ways of white folks throughout his life. When added to her other skills, this irony proves formidable. "The Lovers of the Poor" is unsparing in its portrayal of ineffectual, middle-age, elitist philanthropy:

> Their guild is giving money to the poor.
> The worthy poor. The very very worthy
> And beautiful poor. Perhaps just not too swarthy.
> Perhaps just not too dirty nor too dim
> Nor—passionate. In truth, what they could wish
> Is—something less than derelict or dull.
> Not staunch enough to stab, though, gaze for gaze!
> God shield them sharply from the beggar-bold!

Hughes could not have hoped for better. And the same vitriol is directed at whites who seek the bizarre and exotic by "slumming" among blacks:

> But how shall they tell people they have been
> Out Bronzeville way? For all the nickels in
> Have not bought savagery or defined a "folk."
>
> The colored people will not "clown."
>
> The colored people arrive, sit firmly down,
> Eat their Express Spaghetti, their T-bone steak,
> Handling their steel and crockery with no clatter,
> Laugh punily, rise, go firmly out of the door.
> ("I love those little booths at Benvenuti's")

The poet's chiding, however, is not always in the derisive mode. She often turns an irony of loving kindness on black Americans. "We Real Cool" would fit easily into the canon of Hughes or Sterling Brown:

> We real cool. We
> Left School. We
>
> Lurk late. We
> Strike straight. We
>
> Sing sin. We
> Thin gin. We
>
> Jazz June. We
> Die soon.

[49]

The irony is patent, but the poet's sympathy and admiration for the folk are no less obvious (the bold relief of "We," for example). A sympathetic irony in dealing with the folk has characterized some of the most outstanding works in the black American literary tradition, from Paul Laurence Dunbar's "Jimsella" and the novels of Claude McKay to Ralph Ellison's *Invisible Man* and the work of recent writers such as George Cain and Louise Meriwether. All manifest a concern with the black man living in the "promised land" of the American city, and Miss Brooks's *A Street in Bronzeville, Annie Allen*, "The Bean Eaters," and "Bronzeville Woman in a Red Hat" likewise reveal the employment of kindly laughter to veil the tears of a desperate situation. In her autobiography, *Report From Part One*, she attests to having been in the situation and to having felt its deeper pulsations: "I lived on 63rd Street [in Chicago] . . . and there was a good deal of life in the raw all about me. You might feel that this would be disturbing, but it was not. It contributed to my writing progress. I wrote about what I saw and heard in the street."

Finally, there are the poems of protest. A segregated military establishment comes under attack in both "The Negro Hero" and "the white troops had their orders but the Negroes looked like men." The ignominies of lynching are exposed in "A Bronzeville Mother Loiters in Mississippi. Meanwhile, a Mississippi Mother Burns Bacon." And in poems like "Riders to the Blood-red Wrath" and "The Second Sermon on the Warpland," Miss Brooks expresses the philosophy of militant resistance that has characterized the black American literary tradition from the day a black slave first sang of Pharaoh's army. The poet, in short, has spoken forcefully against the indignities suffered by black Americans in a racialistic society. Having undertaken a somewhat thorough revaluation of her role as a black poet in an era of transition, she has stated and proved her loyalty to the task of creating a new consciousness in her culture. Her shift from a major white publishing firm to an independent black one (Broadside Press) for her autobiography is an indication of her commitment to the cause of black institution building which has been championed by a number of today's black artists. One might, however, take issue with her recent statement that she was "ignorant" until enlightened by the black activities and concerns of the 1960s.

Although she is currently serving as one of the most engaged artistic guides for a culture, she is more justly described as a herald than as an uninformed convert. She has mediated the dichotomy that left Paul Laurence Dunbar (whose *Complete Poems* she read at an early age) a torn and agonized man. Of course, she had the example of Dunbar, the Harlem Renaissance writers, and others to build upon, but at times even superior talents have been incapable of employing the accomplishments of the past for their own ends. Unlike the turn-of-the-century poet and a number of Renaissance writers, Miss Brooks has often excelled the surrounding white framework, and she has been able to see clearly beyond it to the strengths and beauties of her own unique cultural tradition.

Gwendolyn Brooks represents a singular achievement. Beset by a double consciousness, she has kept herself from being torn asunder by crafting poems that equal the best in the black and white American literary traditions. Her characters are believable, her themes manifold, and her technique superb. The critic (whether black or white) who comes to her work seeking only support for his ideology will be disappointed for, as Etheridge Knight pointed out, she has ever spoken the truth. And truth, one likes to feel, always lies beyond the boundaries of any one ideology. Perhaps Miss Brooks's most significant achievement is her endorsement of this point of view. From her hand and fertile imagination have come volumes that transcend the dogma on either side of the American veil. In their transcendence, they are fitting representatives of an "Effulgent lover of the Sun!"

VI

Journey Toward Black Art:
Jean Toomer's *Cane*

WILLIAM Stanley Braithwaite's "The Negro in American Literature," concludes with the rhapsodic assertion that "*Cane* is a book of gold and bronze, of dusk and flame, of ecstasy and pain, and Jean Toomer is a bright morning star of a new day of the race in literature."[1] Written in 1924, Braithwaite's statement reflects the energy and excess, the vibrancy and hope of a generation of young black authors who set out in the 1920s to express their "individual dark-skinned selves without fear or shame."[2] They were wooed by white patrons; they had their work modified beyond recognition by theatrical producers, and they were told time and again precisely what type of black American writing the public would accept. Some, like Wallace Thurman, could not endure the strain.[3] Claude McKay absented himself from Harlem throughout most of the twenties,[4] and Langston Hughes and Countee Cullen gained a degree of notoriety.[5] Ironically, it was *Cane* (1923), a book written by a very light-complexioned mulatto, that portrayed—without fear or shame—a dark-skinned self that transcended the concerns of a single period and

[53]

heralded much of value that has followed its publication. Arna Bontemps writes:

> Only two small printings were issued, and these vanished quickly. However, among the most affected was practically an entire generation of young Negro writers then just beginning to emerge; their reaction to Toomer's *Cane* marked an awakening that soon thereafter began to be called a Negro Renaissance.[6]

The 1920s presented a problem for the writer who wished to give a full and honest representation of black American life; for him the traditional images, drawn from the authors of the Plantation Tradition and the works of Paul Laurence Dunbar, were passé. The contemporary images, captured in Carl Van Vechten's *Nigger Heaven* (1926) and Claude McKay's *Home to Harlem* (1928), were not designed to elucidate a complex human existence, for they were reflections of that search for the bizarre and the exotic that was destined to flourish in an age of raccoon coats, bathtub gin, and "wine-flushed, bold-eyed" whites who caught the A-train to Harlem and spent an evening slumming, or seeking some *élan vital* for a decadent but prosperous age. That only two small printings of *Cane* appeared during the 1920s is not striking: the miracle is that it was published at all. Toomer did not choose the approbation that a scintillating (if untrue) portrayal of the black man could bring in the twenties, nor did he speak *sotto voce* about the amazing progress the black man had made in American society and his imminent acceptance by a fond white world. *Cane* is a symbolically complex work that employs lyrical intensity and stream-of-consciousness narration to portray the journey of an artistic soul toward creative fulfillment; it is unsparing in its criticism of the inimical aspects of the black American heritage and resonant in its praise of the spiritual beauty to be discovered there. An examination of the journey toward genuine, liberating black art presented in *Cane* reveals Toomer as a writer of genius and the book itself as a protest novel, a portrait of the artist, and a thorough delineation of the black situation. These aspects of the work explain its signal place among the achievements of the Harlem Renaissance, and they help to clarify the reaction of a white reading public—a public nurtured on the minstrel tradition, the tracts of the

New Negro, and the sensational antics of Carl Van Vechten's blacks —which allowed it to go out of print without a fair hearing.°

II

The first section of *Cane* opens with evocative description and a lyrical question. The subject is Karintha, whose:

. . . skin is like dusk on the eastern horizon,
O cant you see it, O cant you see it,
Her skin is like dusk on the eastern horizon
. . . When the sun goes down.[7]

The repetition and the simile bringing together the human and the nonhuman leave a memorable impression. The reader is directly asked to respond, as were the hearers of such spirituals as "I've Got a Home in Dat Rock": "Rich man Dives he lived so well/Don't you see?" From the outset, the atmosphere is one of participation, as the reader is invited to contemplate a woman who carries "beauty, perfect as dusk when the sun goes down."

"Karintha," however, offers more than rhapsodic description and contemplation. It is a concise, suggestive sketch of the maturation of a southern woman: from sensuous childhood through promiscuous adolescence to wanton adulthood. The quatrain that serves as the epigraph is repeated twice and acts as a sharp counter-

°Having received a tendentious report from one reader of the following essay, who asserted that "what Baker means by black art is never defined," I thought immediately of a Louis Armstrong anecdote. After one of Satchmo's hottest and most exciting concerts, a young white reporter ran up to the master and said: "Mr. Armstrong, Mr. Armstrong, can you give me a definition of successful jazz?" Wiping his brow and flashing his engaging smile, Satchmo replied: "Man if you don't know now, you'll never know!" Anecdotes aside, let me say that by black art I mean those aesthetic products crafted by individuals who are consciously (even, at times, self-consciously) aware of their Afro-American ancestry and longstanding cultural traditions. The artist's awareness leads him to embody the significant experiences of his culture in expressive form in order that those who share the same ancestry and traditions may recognize themselves and move toward fruitful self-definition. The cognitive and affective responses on the part of the audience are not envisioned as exclusively passive or spiritual experiences. The process of self-definition involves concrete action, i.e., the overthrow of the oppressive, that which blocks an individual's development in accordance with the most humane and effective values of his *sui generis* culture. Toomer's narrator is, thus, an individual who moves toward a fulfillment of the role of black artist, and *Cane* as a whole offers an example of black art.

[55]

point to Karintha's life, which is anything but beautiful: "She stoned the cows, and beat her dog, and fought the other children . . ." In a sense, "Karintha" is a prose "The Four Stages of Cruelty," and its exquisite style forces some of its more telling revelations into a type of Hogarthian background, where they are lost to the casual observer.

There are elements of the humorous black preacher tale in the narrator's comment that "even the preacher, who caught her at mischief, told himself that she was as innocently lovely as a November cotton flower," and grim paradox appears after Karintha has given birth to her illegitimate child near the smoldering sawdust pile of the mill:

> Weeks after Karintha returned home the smoke was so heavy you tasted it in water. Someone made a song:
>> Smoke is on the hills. Rise up.
>> Smoke is on the hills, O rise
>> And take my soul to Jesus.

The holy song that accompanies an unholy event is no less incongruous than the pilgrimages and the fierce, materialistic rituals in which men engage to gain access to Karintha. For the heroine is not an enshrined beauty but a victim of the South, where "homes . . . are most often built on the two room plan. In one, you cook and eat, in the other you sleep, and there love goes on." Karintha has been exposed to an adult world too soon, and the narrator drives home the irony that results when biblical dictates are juxtaposed with a bleak reality: "Karintha had seen or heard, perhaps she had felt her parents loving. One could but imitate one's parents, for to follow them was the way of God." While some men "do not know that the soul of her was a growing thing ripened too soon," the narrator is aware that Karintha has been subjected to conditions that Christianity is powerless to meliorate. Her life has been corrupted, and the mystery is that her beauty remains.

The type of duality instanced by Karintha's sordid life and striking appearance recurs in Part One and lends psychological point to the section.[8] The essential theme of "Karintha" is the debasement of innocence. Men are attracted to the heroine but fail to appreciate what is of value—the spirituality inherent in her dusky beauty. They

[56]

are awed by the pure yet wish to destroy it; evil becomes their good, and they think only in terms of progressive time and capitalistic abundance—"The young fellows counted the time to pass before she would be old enough to mate with them" and ran stills to make her money. These conditions result, in part, from a southern Manichaeanism; for the land whose heritage appears in "Karintha" stated its superiority and condoned an inhumane slavery, spoke of its aristocracy and traded in human flesh, lauded its natural resources and wantonly destroyed them to acquire wealth. Good and evil waged an equal contest in a South that contained its own natural harmonies but considered blacks as chattels personal, bound by no rights that a white man need respect. In such an instance, love could only be an anomaly, and the narrator of Part One seems fully aware of this. When black women are considered property (the materialism surrounding Karintha and Fern) and white women goddesses (the recrimination that accompanies Becky's sacrilegious acts), deep relationships are impossible; the evil of the encompassing universe and the natural compulsion of man to corrupt the beautiful inform the frustrating encounters of Part One.

The two poems—"Reapers" and "November Cotton Flower"—that follow "Karintha" offer a further treatment of the significant themes found in the story. The expectations raised by the title of the first poem are almost totally defeated by its text. There are sharpened blades, black men, black horses, and an inexorable energy; but wearying customs, indifference, and death are also present. "I see them place the hones/In their hip-pockets as a thing that's done," the speaker says, and goes on to depict the macabre death of a field rat that, "startled, squealing bleeds." This event does not halt the movement of the cutters, however: "I see the blade,/ Blood-stained, continue cutting. . . ." An abundant harvest is not the result of the poem's action, and the black reapers, with scythes in hand, take on the appearance of medieval icons of death—an appropriate image for those who help to corrupt the life of Karintha. "November Cotton Flower" with its images of scarcity, drought, dead birds, and boll weevils continues the portrayal of a grim environment. Against this background, however, stands a beauty like Karintha's. The heroine of the first sketch was compared to a November cotton flower, and here the appearance of the "innocently lovely" flower brings about the speculation of the superstitious. "Beauty so sudden for that time of year," one suspects, is destined to attract its exploiters.

While exploring the nature of Karintha's existence, the author has been constructing the setting that is to appear throughout Part One. The first story's effect is heightened by the presence of the religious, the suggestive, and the feminine, and certain aspects of the landscape linger in the reader's mind: a sawmill, pine trees, red dust, a pyramidal sawdust pile, and rusty cotton stalks. The folk songs convey a feeling of cultural homogeneity; they are all of a religious character, rising spontaneously and pervading the landscape. The finishing details of this setting—the Dixie Pike and the railroad—are added in "Becky," which deals with a mode of interaction characteristic of primitive, homogeneous societies.

"Becky" is the story of a white woman who gives birth to two mulatto sons, thus violating one of the most rigid taboos of southern society. As a consequence, she is ostracized by the community. William Goede (following the lead of Robert Bone) describes her plight as follows:

> Becky is, like Hester Prynne, made to pay for the collective sense of guilt of the community: after whites and Negroes exile her, they secretly build her a house which both sustains and finally buries her. The house, on the other hand, built between the road and the railroad, confines the girl until the day when the roof falls through and kills her.[9]

Unlike Karintha, Becky is seldom portrayed in physical terms. The narrator has never seen her, and the community as a whole merely speculates on her actions and her changing appearance. She is primarily a psychological presence to whom the community pays an ironical homage: a spectral representation of the southern miscegenatory impulse that was so alive during the days of American slavery and was responsible for countless lynchings even in Toomer's own day. As early as the seventeenth century, southern legislatures were enacting laws to prevent sexual alliances between blacks and whites; hence, the community in "Becky" reacts in a manner sanctioned by law and custom.

"Becky" presents a further exploration of the duality theme encountered in "Karintha," and here the psychological element seems to predominate. The heroine's exile first calls to mind repression; she is set apart and finally buried. A more accurate description of Becky, however, is that she is a shaman. Among certain Asian groups and American Indian tribes, a person who engages in unsanctioned behavior (homosexuality, for example) is thought to have received a divine summons; he becomes a public figure and devises and leads ritualistic ceremonies that project his abnormal behavior. The function of the shaman is twofold; he enables the community to act out, by proxy, its latent abnormalities, and he reinforces its capacity to resist such tendencies. He is tolerated and revered because of his supernatural power, yet hated as a symbol of moral culpability and as a demanding priest who exacts a penitential toll. The most significant trait of the shaman, however, is that—despite his ascribed powers—he is unable to effect a genuine cure. Georges Devereux explains this paradox:

> Aussie ne peut-on considérer que le chaman accomplit une "cure psychiatrique" au sens *strict* du terme; il procure seulement au malade ce que L'École de psychonalyse de Chicago appelle une "expérience affective corrective" qui l'aide à réorganiser son système de défense mais ne lui permet pas d'attendre à cette réelle prise de conscience de soi-même (*insight*) sans laquelle il n'y a pas de véritable guérison.[10]

It is not surprising that analysts consider the shaman a disturbed individual; he is often characterized by hysteria and suicidal tendencies, and he remains in his role because he finds relief from his own disorders by granting a series of culturally sanctioned defenses to his followers.

Becky has engaged in a pattern of behavior that the surrounding community considers taboo, and she is relegated to a physical position outside the group but essentially public. Her house is built (by the townspeople) in a highly visible location, an "eye-shaped piece of sandy ground. . . . Islandized between the road and railroad track." The citizens scorn her and consider her deranged ("poor-white crazy woman, said the black folks' mouths"), but at the same time they pray for her, bring her food, and keep her alive. Becky, in turn, continues her activities; she has another mulatto son and remains in the tottering house until it eventually crumbles beneath the weight of its chimney. In essence, we witness the same dichotomy presented in "Karintha"; the South professes racial purity and abhorrence of miscegenation, but the fundamental conditions of the region nourish a subconscious desire for interracial relationships and make a penitential ritual necessary. It seems significant, moreover, that Becky—who is a Catholic and in that respect also one of the South's traditional aversions—assumes a divine role for the community. Attraction toward and repulsion by the spiritually ordained are as much a part of the landscape in "Becky" as in "Karintha."

The narrator is swayed by the attitudes of the townspeople, but he is by no means a devout shamanist. He duly records the fact that Becky's house was built on "sandy ground" (reflecting the destructive and aggressive feelings that are part of the shamanic experience), and he points out that Becky is a Catholic. Moreover, he sets up a contrapuntal rhythm between the natural pines that "whisper to Jesus" and the ambivalent charity of the community. The most devastating note in this orchestration is that Sunday is the day of Becky's destruction, and the vagrant preacher Barlo is unwilling to do more than toss a Bible on the debris that entraps her. In short, the narrator captures the irony inherent in the miscegenatory under-consciousness of the South. The town's experience with Becky provides a "corrective, affective experience" but not a substantive cure; as the story closes (on notes that remind one of the eerie conjure stories of black folklore), one suspects that the townspeople are no more insightful.

At this point, Toomer has set forth the dominant tone, setting, characters, and point of view of the first section. Women are in the forefront, and in both "Karintha" and "Becky" they assume symbolic roles that help to illustrate the dualities of a southern heritage. The beauty of Karintha and the beneficent aspects of Becky's existence are positive counterpoints to the aggressiveness, materialism, and moral obtuseness of the community as a whole. The omnipresent folk songs and the refrain in the second story bespeak a commitment to spirituality and beauty, while the animosity of the townspeople in "Becky" and the ineffectiveness of Christianity in "Karintha" display the grimmer side of a lyrically described landscape whose details pervade the whole of *Cane*. The point of view is largely that of a sensitive narrator, whom Arna Bontemps describes:

[60]

Drugged by beauty "perfect as dusk when the sun goes down," lifted and swayed by folk song, arrested by eyes that "desired nothing that *you* could give," silenced by "corn leaves swaying, rusty with talk," he recognized that "the Dixie Pike has grown from a goat path in Africa." A native richness is here, he concluded, and the poet embraced it with the passion of love.[11]

The narrator speaks in a tone that combines awe and reverence with effective irony and subtle criticism. There are always deeper levels of meaning beneath his highly descriptive surface, and this is not surprising when one considers Toomer's statement that in the South "one finds soil in the sense that the Russians know it—the soil every art and literature that is to live must be embedded in."[12]

The emblematic nature of the soil is reflected in the tone and technique of the narrator and particularly in the book's title. Throughout Part One there is an evocation of a land of sugar cane whose ecstasy and pain are rooted in a communal soil. But the title conveys more than this. Justifications of slavery on scriptural grounds frequently traced the black man's ancestry to the race of Cain, the slayer of Abel, in the book of Genesis. Toomer is concerned not only with the Southern soil but also with the sons of Cain who populate it. In a colloquial sense, "to raise Cain" is to create disorder and cacophony, and in a strictly denotative sense, a cane is an instrument of support. Toomer's narrator is attempting to create an ordered framework that will contain the black American's complex existence, offer supportive values, and act as a guide for the perceptive soul's journey from amorphous experience to a finished work of art.

The third story of Part One, "Carma," is called by the narrator "the crudest melodrama," and so it is—on one level. When Carma's husband, Bane (surely an ironical name to set against *karma*), discovers that she has been unfaithful, he slashes the man who has told him, and is sentenced to the chain gang. This is melodramatic to be sure, but only (to quote the narrator) "as I have told it." Beneath the sensational surface is a tragedy of black American life. Bane, like Jimboy in Langston Hughes's *Not Without Laughter,* is forced by economic pressures to seek work away from home; thus, his wife is left alone in an environment where (again, according to the narrator) promiscuity is a norm.[13] But Carma is also a woman who flaunts her sensuality, and can hardly be said to possess a strong sense of responsibility.

As in the previous stories, there are positive and redeeming elements in "Carma." The heroine herself is "strong as any man," and, given her name, this at least implies that her spirituality—that which is best and most ineffable in her—is capable of enduring the inimical aspects of her surroundings. This is particularly important when one considers that "Carma" introduces a legendary African background to the first section: "Torches flare . . juju men, greegree, witch-doctors . . torches go out. . . The Dixie Pike has grown from a goat path in Africa" (pp. 17-18). The passage that introduces this reflection reads: "From far away, a sad strong song. Pungent and composite, the smell of farmyards is the fragrance of the woman. She does not sing; her body is a song. She is in the forest, dancing" (p. 17). The folk song is linked to the African past, and a feeling of cultural continuity is established. The atavistic remains of a ceremonial past have the fragrance of earth and the spirituality of song and dance to recommend them, and at the center of this drama is Carma. She is strong (as Karintha is beautiful) despite southern conditions, and she endures in the face of an insensitive Bane, who is enraged because he cannot master his destiny.

"Carma" is also the first story in which the narrator clearly identifies himself as a conscious recounter ("whose tale as I have told it"), and the poems that follow read like invocations to the heritage that he is exploring. "Song of the Son" states his desire to sing the "souls of slavery," and "Georgia Dusk," which makes further use of the legendary background encountered in "Carma," evokes the spirits of the "unknown bards" of the past. It is not surprising, then, that the story of Fern should follow.

Fern is a woman whom men used until they realized there was nothing they could do for her that would modify her nature or bring them peace. She is an abandoned Karintha, and in a sense a more beautiful and alluring Esther, staring at the world with haunting eyes. The narrator seeks out this beautiful exile who is free in her sexuality and unmoved by the all-pervasive cash nexus of her environment. However, when he asks himself the question posed by former suitors—"What could I do for her?"—his answer is that of

[62]

the artist: "Talk, of course. Push back the fringe of pines upon new horizons" (p. 29). The others answered in solely materialistic terms, coming away from their relationships with Fern oblivious to her fundamental character and vowing to do greater penitence: "candy every week . . . a magnificent something with no name on it . . . a house . . . rescue her from some unworthy fellow who had tricked her into marrying him" (pp. 25-26). The narrator, on the other hand, aspires to project a vision that will release Fern from her stifling existence; she thus becomes for him an inspiration, an artistic ideal. She is a merger of black American physical attractiveness and the unifying myth so important in black American history and in the creation of the spirituals.

"If you have heard a Jewish cantor sing, if he has touched you and made your own sorrow seem trivial when compared with his, you will know my [the narrator's] feeling when I follow the curves of her profile, like mobile rivers, to their common delta," and Fern's full name is Fernie May Rosen. The narrator is thus making use of the seminal comparison between the history of the Israelites and that of black America, which frequently appears in the religious lore of black American culture. In effect, the slaves appropriated the myth of the Egyptian captivity and considered themselves favored by God and destined in time to be liberated by His powers; this provided unity for a people who found themselves uprooted and defined by whites—historians and others—as descendants of wild savages on the "dark continent" of Africa.[14] Despite the fact that she dislikes the petty people of the South and apparently needs to express an underlying spirituality, Fern seems to act as a symbolic representation of the black man's adoption of this myth. When the narrator has brought about a hysterical release from her, however, he fails to comprehend what he has evoked. The story ends with an injunction to the reader to seek out Fern when he travels South. The narrator feels that his ideal holds significance, but that his aspirations toward it are unfulfilled. There is some naivety in this assumption; for the teller of Fern's story has explored the ironies inherent in the merger of white religion and black servitude. The religion of the Israelites is out of place in the life of Fern. While she captures—in her mysterious song like that of a Jewish cantor—the beauty of its spirit (and, in this

[63]

sense, stands outside the narrow-minded community), she is imprisoned by the mores it occasions. Like Becky and Karintha, Fern is a victim, and the narrator skillfully captures her essence. The apparent naivety at the story's conclusion is in reality an act of modesty; for the art the narrator implies is humble actually holds great significance (in its subtle didactic elements) for the culture he is attempting to delineate.

"Esther" is a story of alienation and brings an inquietude that grows into the concluding terror of the book's first section. Apocalyptic images abound as the heroine dreams of King Barlo (a figure who first appeared in "Becky") overcoming her pale frigidity with a flaming passion that will result in a "black, singed, woolly, tobacco-juice baby—ugly as sin" (p. 41). Edward Waldron points out that "beneath this superficial level . . . lie at least two more intense and, for Toomer, more personal interpretations. One deals with the relationship of a light-skinned American Negro to the black community in which he (she) must try to function, and the other has to do with a common theme of the Harlem Renaissance, the relationship between the American Negro and Africa."[15] But one can make excessive claims for King Barlo. While it is true that he falls into a religious trance and sketches, in symbolic oratory, the fate of Africans at the hands of slave traders, it is also true that he is a vagrant preacher, a figure whom Toomer sketches fully (and with less than enthusiasm) in Layman of "Kabnis." And though Barlo is the prophet of a new dawn for the black American, he is also a businessman[16] who makes money during the war, and a lecherous frequenter of the demimonde. It thus seems an overstatement to make a one-to-one corrleation between Barlo and Africa, or Afro-America. It is necessary to bear in mind that Esther Crane is not only a "tragic mulatto" repressed by Protestant religion and her father's business ethic ("Esther sells lard and snuff and flour to vague black faces that drift in her store to ask for them"), she is a fantasizer as well. Esther's view of Barlo is the one presented to the reader through most of the story; hence, when she retreats fully from reality at the conclusion, the reader's judgments should be qualified accordingly.

Esther's final state is described as follows: "She draws away, frozen. Like a somnambulist she wheels around and walks stiffly to the stairs. Down them. . . . She steps out. There is no air, no street, and the town has completely disappeared" (p. 48). The heroine is enclosed in her own mind; the sentient objects of the world mean nothing to this repressed sleepwalker. Given the complexity of Barlo's character, it is impossible to feel that such an observer could capture it accurately. Just as we refuse to accept the middle-aged and sentimental reflections of Marlowe as the final analysis of Kurtz in Conrad's "Heart of Darkness" and exercise a qualifying restraint before the words of Camus' narrator in *The Fall,* so we must recognize the full nature of Esther's character if we are to grasp her story and the role of King Barlo in it. Barlo does contain within himself the unifying myth of black American culture, and he delivers it to the community in the manner of the most accomplished black folk preachers. In this character, however, he paradoxically contributes to Esther's stifled sensibility, which continually projects visions of sin. As a feat hero (the best cotton picker) and a skillful craftsman of words (his moving performance on the public street), he contains positive aspects, but the impression that remains—when one has noted his terrified and hypocritical response in "Becky" and his conspicuous materialism and insensitive treatment of Esther—is not as favorable as some critics would tempt us to believe.[17]

The feelings of alienation and foreshadowing generated by "Esther" are heightened by the poems that follow. "Conversion" tells of a degraded "African Guardian of Souls" who has drunkenly yielded place to white religiosity, and seems intended to further enlighten the character of Barlo. "Portrait in Georgia" is a subtle, lyrical protest poem in which a woman is described in terms of the instruments and actions of a lynching. The second poem's vision prefigures the horror of the last story in Part One, "Blood-Burning Moon."

"Blood-Burning Moon" stands well in the company of such Harlem Renaissance works as Claude McKay's "If We Must Die" and Walter White's *The Fire in the Flint.* It is a work that protests, in unequivocal terms, the senseless, brutal, and sadistic violence perpetrated against the black man by white America. The narrator realized in "Carma" that violence was a part of southern existence, and the shattering demise of Becky, Barlo's religious trance, and Fern's frantic outpouring speak volumes about the terror of such a life. But in "Blood-Burning Moon" the narrator traces southern violence to its source. Tom Burwell—strong, dangerous, black lover of Louisa and second to Barlo in physical prowess—is only one of the black Americans whom the Stone family "practically owns." Louisa—black and alluring—works for the family, and Bob Stone (who during the days of slavery would have been called "the young massa") is having an affair with her. Tom reacts to hints and rumors of this affair in the manner of Bane; he turns violently on the gossipers and refuses to acknowledge what he feels to be true. Wage slavery, illicit alliances across the color line, intraracial violence—the narrator indeed captures the soul of America's "peculiar institution," and the results are inevitable. In a confrontation between Stone and Burwell, the black man's strength triumphs, and the white mob arrives (in "high-powered cars with glaring search-lights" that remind one of the "ghost train" in "Becky") to begin its gruesome work. The lynching of Tom, which drives Louisa insane, more than justifies the story's title. The moon, controller of tides and destinies, and a female symbol, brings blood and fire to the black American.

Part One is a combination of awe-inspiring physical beauty, human hypocrisy, restrictive religious codes, and psychological trauma. In "Fern" the narrator says: "That the sexes were made to mate is the practice of the South" (p. 26). But sexual consummation in the first section often results in dissatisfaction or in a type of perverse motherhood. Men come away from Fern frustrated; Karintha covertly gives birth to her illegitimate child in a pine forest; Esther dreams of the immaculate conception of a tobacco-stained baby, and Becky's sons are illegitimate mulattoes, who first bring violence to the community then depart from it with curses. The women of Part One are symbolic figures, but the lyrical terms in which they are described can be misleading. With the exception of their misdirected sexuality, they are little different from the entrapped and stifled women of the city seen in Part Two. In short, something greater than the pressure of urban life accounts for the black man's frustrated ambitions, violent outbursts, and tragic deaths at the hands of white America. The black American's failure to fully comprehend the beautiful in his own heritage—the Georgia landscape, folk songs, and women of deep loveliness—is part of it. But the narrator places even greater emphasis on the black man's ironical acceptance of the "strange cassava" and "weak palabra" of a white religion. Throughout Part One, he directs pointed thrusts—in the best tradition of David Walker, Frederick Douglass, and William Wells Brown[18]—at Christianity. Although he appreciates the rich beauty of black folk songs that employ Protestant religious imagery ("Georgia Dusk"), he also sees that the religion as it is practiced in the South is often hypocritical and stifling. The narrator, as instanced by "Nullo," the refrain in "Becky" ("The pines whisper to Jesus"), and a number of fine descriptive passages throughout the first section, seems to feel a deeper spirituality in the landscape. Moreover, there seems more significance in the beauty of Karintha or in the eyes of Fern (into which flow "the countryside and something that I call God") than in all the cramped philanthropy, shouted hosannas, vagrant preachers, and religious taboos of Georgia. The narrator, in other words, clearly realizes that the psychological mimicry that led to the adoption of a white religion often directed black Americans away from their own spiritual beauties and resulted in destruction.[19]

But the importance of white America's role cannot be minimized. King Barlo views the prime movers behind the black situation as "little white-ant biddies" who tied the feet of the African, uprooted him from his traditional culture, and made him prey to alien gods. The essential Manichaeanism of a South that thrived on slavery, segregation, the chattel principle, and violence is consummately displayed in the first section of *Cane*, and Barlo realizes that a new day must come before the black man will be free. The brutality directed against the black American has slowed the approach of such a dawn, but the narrator of Part One has discovered positive elements in the black Southern heritage that may lead to a new day: a sense of song and soil, and the spirit of a people who have their severe limitations but cannot be denied.

III

Part Two of *Cane* is set in the city and constitutes a male cycle. The creative soul that was characterized by a type of "negative capability" in Part One becomes an active agency of dreams and

[67]

knowledge, and the narrator recedes to a more objective plane, where he can view even himself somewhat impartially. "Avey" has a first-person point of view, but the remainder of the stories come from the hand of an omniscient narrator who seems aware that as a creator he needs "consummate skill to walk upon the waters where huge bubbles burst" (p. 108). The urban environment demands more careful analysis, and thus the lyrical impulse is diminished in the second section—there are only half as many connecting poems here as in Part One.

"Seventh Street" and "Rhobert," the opening sketches of Part Two, capture the positive and negative aspects of a new environment. The driving, cutting, inexorable energy seen in "Reapers" and "Cotton Song" has become "A crude-boned, soft-skinned wedge of nigger life" thrusting its way "into the white and white-washed wood of Washington" (p. 71). And the epigraph of the first sketch evokes a lower-echelon black urban environment—with its easy spending, bootleggers, silken shirts, and Cadillacs—not a dusky, natural beauty like Karintha's. The setting, however, is not a bizarre and exotic world; it is a life fathered by the incongruous combination of senseless violence ("the war") and puritan morality ("Prohibition"). Unlike the Southern environment with its African ancestry, Seventh Street is a disharmony of nature—"a bastard"—and its rhythms reflect its cacophonous birth: thrusting, jazzy, crude-boned. They cannot be absorbed by the white world that surrounds them: "Stale soggy wood of Washington. Wedges ruse in soggy wood. . . Split it! In two! Again! Shred it! . . the sun. Wedges are brilliant in sun; ribbons of wet wood dry and blow away" (p. 71). The new life is an agency of the sun rather than the moon, and those who set it to work can neither contain nor arrest it. This situation becomes sardonically humorous when the narrator comments: "God would not dare to suck black red blood. A Nigger God! He would duck his head in shame and call for the Judgment Day." The omnipotent Father (frequently pictured by church primers as a blue-eyed white man) would be irrevocably altered by one drop of black blood. But there are black Americans who fear this new life. They wear their God-built houses like divers' helmets and refuse to subject themselves to its pressures. Rhobert—who might appropriately be called "robot"—is ruled by the white ethical code (the house) that has been imposed upon him.[20] After reading "Rhobert" and "Seventh Street," one is aware that one is in the presence of a narrator who has learned to look intelligently beneath the surface of life. His irony is more subtle, and the near-Swiftian satire of the second sketch demonstrates his ability to make accurate, undisguised value judgments. Moreover, he has moved toward greater self-knowledge; if Rhobert is portrayed as a man engaged in a somewhat fruitless contest, so, too, is the first-person narrator of "Avey."

Goede has pointed out that "Avey," "Box Seat," and "Kabnis" represent portraits of the black American artist,[21] and "Avey's" narrator clearly identifies himself as a writer near the end of the story. Avey, whom Darwin Turner calls "an educated and northern Karintha,"[22] acts as a sensual ideal for the narrator and his boyhood peers; they long to mate with her and seek to give something she desires. Avey, however, is extraordinarily indifferent to them. She pursues an uneventful life and finally becomes a prostitute.

Despite the humor he directs at her indifference ("Hell! she was no better than a cow. I was certain that she was a cow when I felt an udder in a Wisconsin stock-judging class"), Avey becomes an artistic ideal for the narrator. Having seen her, he cannot forget her and longs to do something for her. Unlike the setting of "Fern," the backdrop for the narrator's quest in "Avey" is not in harmony with his designs: V Street in Washington's black community, an amusement park, the Potomac River, Harpers Ferry, and Soldier's Home; and the sounds that rise from this landscape are not resonant folk songs: "The engines of this valley have a whistle, the echoes of which sound like iterated gasps and sobs. I always think of them as crude music from the soul of Avey" (p. 81).

At the outset of "Avey," the narrator comments:

> I like to think now that there was a hidden purpose in the way we [he and his childhood friends] hacked them [boxes on V Street containing saplings] with our knives. I like to feel that something deep in me responded to the trees, the young trees that whinnied like colts impatient to be let free. . . . (P. 76)

[69]

As the story progresses, the manner in which he hopes to bestow freedom becomes less violent, and in his last encounter with Avey, he (as in "Fern") conceives of talk as artistic expression, as an agency of liberation:

> I talked, beautifully I thought, about an art that would be born, an art that would open the way for women the likes of her. I asked her to hope, and build up an inner life against the coming of that day. I recited some of my own things to her. I sang, with a strange quiver in my voice, a promise-song. (P. 87)

But while the narrator evoked, at least, a hysterical response from Fern, he finds Avey asleep when he has finished talking. He realizes finally that Avey's is not the type of loveliness that characterizes a new day: "She did not have the gray crimson-splashed beauty of the dawn."

Bone ventures the idea that "Toomer's intellectualizing males are tragic because they value talking above feeling,"[23] but such a formulation implies that beautiful talk and profound feelings are mutually exclusive in *Cane*, which is not the case. The narrator derides himself for having "dallied dreaming" instead of making advances to Avey during a youthful holiday, and he realizes the absurdity of his situation when he finds her asleep. However, he also depicts himself as a man with his mind "set on freedom" and knows that art can play a role in achieving this end. Moreover, he is the character who evokes that sense of song and soil that received such positive valuations in Part One. He describes the setting for his final meeting with Avey as follows: "And when the wind is from the South, soil of my homeland falls like a fertile shower upon the lean streets of the city." And during the encounter, he reflects: "I wanted the Howard Glee Club to sing 'Deep River, Deep River,' from the road." The glee club's song is proposed as a substitute for the tinny, regimental music of the band, just as the narrator's dreams and visions are posed as liberating forces for the life of Avey. The feeling of frustration that concludes the story, therefore, does not result totally from a flaw in the narrator's character, but also from the intractability of his artistic materials. Avey, who is one of the more languorous and promiscuous members of the new urban black bourgeoisie, is hopelessly insensible to the artist's rendering of "a larger life," and one would scarcely expect her to respond to a beautiful heritage. She is, indeed, an "orphan-woman."

In the poems "Beehive" and "Storm Ending," the narrator first views the "black hive" as a place where he can rest indifferently, taking his pleasures in the manner of Avey. He soon realizes, however, that "Earth is a waxen cell of the world comb" and longs to move outward toward greater fulfillment—"And curl forever in some far-off farmyard flower." The images of pleasure in "Beehive" are transmuted to ones of disharmony in "Storm Ending." Honey becomes rain, and flowers appear as ominous thunder from which the earth flees. Together, the poems seem to offer a further comment on "Avey." While Avey is alluring and a member of that class of blacks who (during Toomer's day) sought their alliances among college-bred men and women, she is unable (or unwilling) to respond to the beauties of her heritage. She cannot listen with interest to the narrator's evocations of the past or to his idealistic projections of a future black American creativity that will release men from their stifling existence. There is not only insensitivity in Avey's reaction but also a kind of tragedy, since it makes her an even greater victim of the urban anonymity and disharmony that confronted so many blacks after their migration from the South to the North at the beginning of the twentieth century. Hence, the transvaluation of images that occurs between "Beehive" and "Storm Ending" offers another instance of the duality theme; when one has penetrated the cardboard masks labeled "progress" and "the New Negro," one is likely to find the same obliviousness to life and to society's deeper meanings that appears repeatedly in Part One.

With the exception of "Bona and Paul," the stories and poems that follow "Storm Ending" in Part Two are restatements of concerns that have been treated earlier. The protagonists of "Theater" and "Box Seat" are both dreamers who envision passionate affairs with women bound by convention. Dorris in "Theater," like Muriel in "Box Seat," dances with energy, but neither could conceive of saying, in Imamu Baraka's words,

I want to be sung. I want
all my bones and meat hummed

[71]

against the thick floating
winter sky. I want myself
as dance. As what I am
given love, or time, or space
to feel myself.[24]

Dorris uses her dance, which is "of Canebreak loves and mangrove feastings," to solicit from John silk stockings and "kids, and a home, and everything," which she equates with love. And Muriel, after attracting Dan with her dance, is too repressed by societal dictates (represented by "Mrs. Pribby," a name second only to "Mrs. Grundy" in its devastating effects) to accept his love and his vision of life.

Of course, John and Dan have severe shortcomings. John's being, like the speaker's in "Prayer" and the woman's in "Calling Jesus," is fragmented. Dan suffers from a romantic megalomania that leads him to believe he is a type of the new Messiah. But while one can imagine either engaging in the stilted, "bower of bliss" romance described in "Her Lips Are Copper Wire" or in the fruitless self-indulgence of "Harvest Song," both are characters who possess the ability to dream and project rejuvenating images drawn from the black American heritage. John feels himself become the "mass-heart" of the black urban folk (p. 92), and he envisions a Dorris —"Her face is tinted like the autumn alley. Of old flowers, or of a southern canefield, her perfume." (p. 99)—who could share his artistic dreams: "John reaches for a manuscript and reads" (p. 99). In "Box Seat," the narrator's injunction to the "gleaming limbs and asphalt torso" of the street might well have been directed to Dan Moore:

> Shake your curled wool-blossoms, nigger. Open your liver lips to the lean, white spring. Stir the root-life of a withered people. Call them from their houses, and teach them to dream. (P. 104)

The dream is one of the most important elements in the second section; it can reunify the body and the soul separated by northern life ("Calling Jesus"), and it can stir the "root-life" of black Americans given to the mindless pleasures (the popular theater or Crimson Gardens) of the city and hemmed in by its rigid structures—moral codes, box seats, boxes, houses. The artist may be affected by the

[72]

malaise of urban life, and as a consequence he may withdraw so
far from it that his imaginative vision fragments the self (like John's
in "Theater"), obscuring the physical beauty before him (Dorris's
dance)—but he is the bringer of dreams.

The whole of Part Two might justifiably be called a portrait of
the artist who has been removed from a primitive and participatory
culture to suffer the alienation of modern life. One means of overcoming this estrangement is the dream, which calls forth positive
images from the past; but when the artist's reveries become—for
any reason—simply acts of self-indulgence (a word that might de-
scribe John's imaginings), he must move beyond the dream in a
search for greater self-knowledge and a broader definition of the
artist's role. The theme of "Bona and Paul," the concluding story of
the second section, involves such a quest. When the story opens,
Paul has become so introspective that his associates are baffled; even
Bona, who is white (reviving the miscegenation theme of "Becky"
and "Blood-Burning Moon"), though attracted to Paul, fails to comprehend him. Action is limited in the story: four students from a
regimented physical education college in Chicago go on a date to
Crimson Gardens. The primary focus of the largely stream-of-consciousness narration is the mind of Paul, which "follows the sun to a
pine-matted hillock in Georgia" (p. 137). The passage following this
description holds significance for "Bona and Paul" and for *Cane* as
a whole:

> He sees the slanting roofs of gray unpainted cabins tinted lavender. A
> Negress chants a lullaby beneath the mate-eyes of a southern planter.
> Her breasts are ample for the suckling of a song. She weans it, and sends
> it, curiously weaving, among lush melodies of cane and corn. Paul fol-
> lows the sun into himself in Chicago. (P. 138)

The essence of the black southern heritage is in Paul's dream, but
what is more important is that the dreamer incorporates the sun of
this heritage into himself: "He is at Bona's window. With his own
eyes he looks through a dark pane." Bona contains no light, and Art,
Paul's roommate, "is like the electric light which he snaps on." At
Crimson Gardens the illumination is artificial. Paul, whom Bona
designates "a poet—or a gym instructor," becomes a source of natural
light, and he is neither a lyric poet like the speaker of "Reapers,"

nor a regimented victim of "mental concepts" like the drillers seen at the beginning of the story. He has transcended a narrowly personal stage of art and moves toward a stance as the knowing, philosophical creator. His epiphany occurs at Crimson Gardens:

> Suddenly he knew that people saw, not attractiveness in his dark skin, but difference. Their stares, giving him to himself, filled something long empty within him, and were like green blades sprouting in his consciousness. There was fullness, and strength and peace about it all. He saw himself, cloudy, but real. (P. 145)

Paul turns first to a brief exploration of the white world, which he finds lovely in its artificial light. He dances with Bona, and passion flares for an instant. The couple leaves the garden. But night is alien to Bona:

> Perhaps for some reason, white skins are not supposed to live at night. Surely, enough nights would transform them fantastically, or kill them. And their red passion? Night paled that too, and made it moony. (P. 141)

When Paul is suddenly possessed by the night and the face of the black doorman (the man outside the garden), Bona realizes that she cannot contain, or comprehend, his desires. The fact that Bona has left when Paul returns does not mean the story's conclusion is pessimistic. Paul has come to greater self-knowledge, and he turns from Bona in an attempt to share it with another black man. The departure of Bona simply reinforces Paul's initial assessment:

> From the South. What does that mean, precisely, except that you'll love or hate a nigger? Thats a lot. What does it mean except that in Chicago you'll have the courage to neither love or hate. A priori. (P. 148)

It is Bona who is cold, imprisoned by the white mental restraints her companion has rejected. Paul is like a nascent black sun and has taken the first step toward sharing his vision with his people.

Part Two, therefore, moves beyond the dream to knowledge:

> I'd like to know you whom I look at. Know, not love. Not that knowing is a greater pleasure; but that I have just found the joy of it. You came just a month too late. Even this afternoon I dreamed. (P. 148)

From the lyrical, awed, contemplative narrator of "Karintha," *Cane* has progressed to a self-conscious, philosophical creator who contains "his own glow" and rejects the artificial garden of white life. "Kabnis," the concluding section of *Cane*, deals with the actions of such an artist vis-à-vis black southern life. It brings the action of the book full circle and completes the portrait of the artist.

IV

The narrator of "Avey" seeks "the simple beauty of another's soul" and "the truth that people bury in their hearts" (pp. 85-86). The artist in "Kabnis," however, searches for knowledge of his own soul and an artistic design that will express it. From the simple observation of the physical beauty of women, the narrator has moved to a fuller exploration of the complexities that beset the black soul. Most of the symbolic figures in the drama are men, and the process of making undisguised value judgments, at work in "Rhobert," is fundamental to "Kabnis." The work is not only a return to the South, but also an open protest (as opposed to the subtle, lyrical criticism dominant in Part One) against its stifling morality and brutal violence.

Though a number of recent critics have insisted that Ralph Kabnis is an unsympathetic character,[25] Bontemps correctly states that the protagonist "is a languishing idealist finally redeemed from cynicism and dissipation by the discovery of underlying strength in his people."[26] And Goede is tellingly accurate when he writes:

> In Kabnis Jean Toomer has discovered an appropriate symbol of the Negro writers who hope to stir "the root-life of a withered people." Like [Ralph] Ellison's hero-writer [in *Invisible Man*], Toomer's hero-writer senses at least the first tentative step toward a commitment, through art, to racial experiences of the Negro.[27]

Ralph Kabnis is a Northerner who has come South to teach. He is fired by Hanby, the school superintendant (and an unctuous counterpart to Mrs. Pribby), and taken in by the wagonsmith, Halsey. Kabnis meets Layman, a southern preacher, and Lewis, a Northerner who has made a contract with himself—presumably to investigate the South for a month. The introspective Kabnis proves a hopeless failure as a manual worker and spends much of his time in

[75]

the cellar of the wagon shop, which is reached by stairs located behind "a junk heap." "Besides being the home of a very old man, . . . [the cellar] is used by Halsey on those occasions when he spices up the life of the small town." The old man is attended by Carrie K. Halsey's sister, and when first encountered he has been mumbling and fasting for two weeks. Halsey arranges a night of debauchery for himself, Kabnis, and Lewis, and the play concludes on the morning afterward, when the old man speaks. As in "Bona and Paul," however, action plays a minor role in "Kabnis"; description, dialogue, and reflection provide the points of focus. The message they render is that the old ethic of the southern black man—composed of Protestantism, vocational education, shopkeeping, and accommodation—will not suffice in a violent white society. Moreover, the new scientific approach to the complexities of black American life, represented by Lewis—whom Goede equates (I think correctly) with an intellectual "race man" such as W. E. B. Du Bois—is unsatisfactory. Kabnis delivers the following thrust at the scientific attitude in general:

> You know, Ralph, old man, it wouldn't surprise me at all to see a ghost. People dont think there are such things. They rationalize their fear, and call their cowardice science. Fine bunch, they are. (P. 165)

Surely this reflection helps to elucidate the later actions of Lewis.

A similarly critical attitude surrounds all those activities of the black American's southern existence which the narrator and the author consider ineffective or inimical. Negative images abound, for example, wherever religion is mentioned:

> God is a profligate red-nosed man about town. Bastardy; me. A bastard son has got a right to curse his maker. (Kabnis, p. 161)

> Above its [the church's] squat tower, a great spiral of buzzards reaches far into the heavens. An ironic comment upon the path that leads into the Christian land. . . (The author, p. 169)

> This preacher-ridden race. Pray and shout. Theyre in the preacher's hands. Thats what it is. And the preacher's hands are in the white man's pockets. (Kabnis, p. 174)

Elsewhere in the story, God is seen as the creator of shopkeepers and moralizers; Layman is portrayed as a reticent vagabond too frightened to speak against the evils of lynching, and the singing and

shouting of a black church service are the backdrop for a chilling story
of mob violence. Negative images also surround Halsey, a descendant
of seven generations of shopkeepers and a man for whom time has
stopped—"an old-fashioned mantelpiece supports a family clock (not
running)" (p. 167). Finally, Lewis—who at different points in "Kabnis" appears as a Christ figure, a race man, and an alter ego for
the protagonist—becomes "a dead chill" when confronted with the
depths of the black southern experience:

> Their pain is too intense. He cannot stand it. He bolts from the table.
> Leaps up the stairs. Plunges through the work-shop and out into the
> night. (P. 226)

The most favorable assessment of Lewis that can be made is that he
seems much like the narrator in "Fern"—an observer awed by the
beauty and pain of the South.

The laudable characters in the play are Kabnis and Carrie K. The
protagonist is the knowing artist who confronts the desert places in
himself, and Carrie K. is the young, chaste ideal of a new art. Both
characters, however, have their limitations. Carrie is constrained by
conventional ethics:

> And then something happens. Her face blanches. Awkwardly she draws
> away. The sin-bogies of respectable southern colored folks clamor at
> her: "Look out! Be a *good* girl. A *good* girl. Look out!" (P. 205)

Kabnis is often self-indulgent, overly ceremonious, and terrified at
the violence of the South. His is a Kurtzian vision, and his mulatto
status (as with Paul and several of the other characters in *Cane*)
comes to represent the gray world of alienation confronting modern
man.

Carrie K. and Kabnis, however, are the individuals who function
most effectively in the cellar, or "the hole," which represents the
collective unconscious of black America. The hole is presided over by
an enthroned figure whom Halsey and Carrie K. call "Father," but
upon whom the awestruck Lewis bestows a religious title, "Father
John." It is finally Kabnis who elicits from the black father his wisdom; the old man denounces: "Th sin whats fixed . . . upon th
white folks . . . f tellin Jesus—lies. O th sin th white folks 'mitted
when they made the Bible lie" (p. 237). Carrie K.'s reaction is one
of tears and tolerance, but Kabnis—as well he might be—is incensed.

For though the old man has condemned the hypocrisy of whites, his vocabulary is one of sin and the Bible. Kabnis, on the other hand, knows that:

> It was only a preacher's sin they [those of John's generation] knew in those old days, an that wasnt sin at all. Mind me, th only sin is whats done against th soul. Th whole world is a conspiracy t sin, especially in America, an against me. . . . I'm what sin is. (P. 236)

The protagonist is aware that a new vocabulary, one that will "fit m soul" and capture that "twisted awful thing that crept in [to my soul] from a dream, a godam nightmare" (p. 224), is needed; the black man must have a new vision of life crafted by the sensitive artist. Black art can function as a new and liberating religion.

The desciption that begins the fifth act of "Kabnis" reinforces this interpretation:

> Night, soft belly of a pregnant Negress, throbs evenly against the torso of the South. Cane—and cotton-fields, pine forests, cypress swamps, saw-mills, and factories are fecund at her touch. Night's womb-song sets them singing. Night winds are the breathing of the unborn child whose calm throbbing in the belly of a Negress sets them somnolently sing-ing. (P. 209)

This imagery is followed by the ritualistic, confessional scenes in the hole, during which Kabnis wears a ceremonial robe; the next morning—in a setting characterized by glowing coals and women who have the beauty of African princesses—Kabnis prostrates himself before John's throne. The tone of the last two acts reflects solemnity, hope, and a new birth. Thus, when John lies expiring in the arms of Carrie K., the scene has the significance of an annunciation. He speaks the words "Jesus Come" in the presence of the woman whom Lewis viewed as a mother figure for Kabnis (p. 208) and who is described by the dramatist as "lovely in her fresh energy of the morning, in the calm untested confidence and nascent maternity which rise from the purpose of her present mission" (p. 233). The con-cluding scene witnesses Kabnis, a new-world creator, ascending from the cellar as the herald and agent of the dawn prophesied by Barlo in "Esther." In his hands are the dead coals of a past ritual, and the expectations generated by the opening of Act Five are fulfilled:

Outside, the sun arises from its cradle in the tree-tops of the forest.
Shadows of pines are dreams the sun shakes from its eyes. The sun
arises. Gold-glowing child, it steps into the sky and sends a birth-song
slanting down gray dust streets and sleepy windows of the southern
town. (P. 239)

The hopes of the narrator in "Song of the Sun" and the aspirations of
the dreaming souls in Part Two will be realized by the initiated
Kabnis, who contains the inner glow of the protagonist in "Bona
and Paul" and has made a successful pilgrimage through the black
heritage to the "souls of slavery."

Kabnis beseeches that he not be tortured with beauty and
goes on to say, "Dear Jesus, do not chain me to myself and set these
hills and valleys, heaving with folk-songs, so close to me that I cannot
reach them" (p. 161). The deeper meanings of the songs have touched
him, and in an early soliloquy that combines the narrator's goals in
Parts One and Two, he says: "If I, the dream (not what is weak and
afraid in me) could become the face of the South. How my lips would
sing for it, my songs being the lips of its soul" (p. 158). He realizes,
however, that there are also inimical aspects of the past and describes them in scathing, oftentimes bitter terms. What distinguishes him from others (like Layman and Halsey, who have seen
the darker side of the South) is his self-awareness; he realizes that
the paranoia, aggressiveness, ambivalence, and hypocrisy of the
South find counterparts in his own personality. One expects, therefore, that a portion of his new art will be devoted to serious intro-
spection. This self-knowledge and independence lead Kabnis to
recognize the profound spirit involved in the creation of the song
that serves as a refrain for the drama, but they also lead him to
protest bitterly the limitations implied by its lyrics:

White-man's land.
Niggers, sing.
Burn, bear black children
Till poor rivers bring
Rest, and sweet glory
In Camp Ground.

Kabnis is the fully emergent artist—a singer of a displaced "soil-
soaked beauty" and an agent of liberation for his people.

[79]

V

Cane led the way in a return to the black folk spirit, which Eugenia Collier has seen as one of the most vital developments of the Harlem Renaissance,[28] and it did so in a form and style that have scarcely been surpassed by subsequent American authors. Toomer knew—and did not attempt to sublimate—the pains and restrictions of a black Southern heritage. This angst is astutely criticized in *Cane* and magnificently portrayed as the somber result of white America's exploitation and oppression, black America's too willing acceptance, and the inherent duality in the nature of man— the Manichaeanism of the universe, emblemized by the southern past—which both marvels at and seeks to destroy beauty. Opposed to "the burden of southern history"—indeed, to the darker side of human history, with its inhibitions, omnipresent violence, and moral ineptitude—however, are the pristine loveliness and indomitable spirit of the folk, to be discovered and extolled by the sensitive observer. A folk culture containing its own resonant harmonies, communal values and assumptions, and fruitful proximity to the ancestral soil offers a starting point for the journey toward black art. The artist, however, cannot simply observe the surface beauties of this culture; he must comprehend the self-knowledge and nobility of spirit that made its creation possible in the midst of an inhuman servitude. Toomer repeatedly asserts this in *Cane*, and at times the book reads like a tragic allegory, posing good against evil, suffering against redemption, hope against despair. As the reader struggles to fit the details together, he becomes increasingly involved in the complexities of the black situation. He moves, in short, toward that freedom that always accompanies deeper self-knowledge and a genuine understanding of one's condition in the universe. In this sense, *Cane* is not only a journey toward liberating black American art but also what philosophy calls the *Ding-an-Sich*—the thing in itself.

VII

From the Inferno to the American Dream:
George Cain's *Blueschild Baby*

GEORGE Cain's *Blueschild Baby* opens on a familiar note:

It is getting dark now and still I roam the corridors of bedlam. I need sanctuary, but there is none, and as my invisibility leaves like a cloak, I feel naked, center of all eyes, fair game for whoever first stumbles across me.[1]

With the introductory description, one has a sense of the novel's referents: the escape-pursuit-capture motif of the slave narratives, the symbolic use of invisibility, and the correlation between the black situation and insanity. Cain, however, immediately defeats traditional expectations by carrying his reader into a world of drug addicts, a lifeless kingdom in which the grotesque gnome, Sun, holds court and parodies the splendors of Louis XIV by selling dope from his bed. The narrator is himself an addict and accepts the values and codes of this inferno with an uneasy grace. The Newark riot serves as a backdrop for the action.

Throughout the first half the narrator's actions are purposeless, and his *carpe diem* existence serves as a vehicle for his journeys to and commentaries on various scenes of black American life. Hopelessness and militancy prevail in this section, and the overriding

[81]

metaphor is one of imprisonment. J. B., the oral historian of the projects, says:

> He's telling us what everyone of us knows but refuses to believe. In this place, we're criminals and treated like. It's like prison, every brother should go. When there, keep expecting to feel different but you don't. Know why? Cause you been in prison all your life. Once you know this, pressure is taken off your brain and you can think, you can do anything cause you got nothing to lose. (P. 35)

All black Americans are trapped by a vast web of circumstances, and their only escapes are senseless diversion and fruitless destruction. Men play dominoes, shoot craps, get high, and fight one another for the excitement of the gallery. Young boys run the streets tossing Molotov cocktails, only to find their communities in ruin and themselves victims of National Guard bullets. The narrator feels caught in this hell. He is anti-heroic and satirical but does not view himself as an exile. Instead, he solipsistically colors his environment, glorifying the actions of the damned. Their insensitivity and limitation are the results of white oppression, and the one crime they have committed is awareness—a realization of their state. Knowing that black America is a penal colony, the occupants have declared a separate state where the expectations of the larger society are inoperative. These premises lead the narrator to romanticize some of the seamier sides of black existence. Lolly, Fat, Sun, Broadway, Sugar, and a number of others become sentient, empathetic characters when seen through his distorting lenses. As one of their number, the narrator seems compelled to justify their patterns of action.

The naturalistic impulses of the first half are neutralized, however, by the narrator's memories of childhood. The city may exert a negative influence on the lives of black Americans, but there are also positive counters. The thought of hard, clean basketball on playground courts is vivid. The tenderness of a mother who was always present to save one from the terrors of an elevator lingers. And the strong communal sense that radiates from the description of Reverend McKenzie's Sunday morning service helps to unify the narrative. There is a harmony in the black urban experience that can be lost to the easily manipulated consciousness. Cain's narrator is ceaselessly moved by the scenes of yesterday and sees more deeply into black city life than those who surround him. While he moves as an observer and participant through moments of deprivation and resignation, poetical flashes of a hidden loveliness and a time of innocence offset his desire to sink calmly into hell. One side of his being pushes him to the next fix while another rebels against the human waste and decay of the spirit that characterize his situation.

He describes his sense of community among pariahs: "As I approach they salute me as comrades do, 'Hey brother,' and the bitches, 'Baby.' We are a fraternity of selflessness, bound together by our communal rejection. We love each other and know it not" (p. 2). But several pages later he speaks of the madness of the city and resorts to atavistic predictions of a day of reckoning:

> We are pushed into a car full of smelling, balky cattle and scream off through the tunnel. The Man cannot stand the cities, the noise drives him mad, silence is his heritage. . . . But we are of tropic jungles where the noise level is intense. . . . We shall not have to kill the Man off. He will do it himself, his system has a built-in suicide mechanism. (P. 46)

Though the narrator says the streets hold him more than any drug and that the "peopled asphalt" is his home, he is basically a man who has accepted his bourgeois tutelage. His aspirations are in harmony with the best aspects of the American dream. He has gone off the track at several points, but the first half of *Blueschild Baby* represents the final phase of his season in hell. The reveries of childhood and first love are much more in keeping with his fundamental personality than all the horror encountered during his drugged journey through the inferno.

J. B., Stacy, and most of those who surround him realize that the narrator stands outside the framework he tries to make home. But George Cain is not one to be molded into "a composite of all their needs and desires" (p. 191). His plight is strikingly akin to that of W. E. B. Du Bois's hero in "Of the Coming of John"[2]; he is the black man of talent whose intellectual prowess has cut him off from his own people. At the same time, he knows that he will never be accepted as an equal by whites. His situation is further complicated by the fact that he falls between the passivist strategies of

[83]

the early sixties, when blacks hoped to move into the mainstream through nonviolence, and the heightened awareness of the late sixties and early seventies, when they unequivocally manifested their dissatisfaction with American society. He gives a sympathetic view of the Muslims and the youngsters who stand black and proud, but he also portrays his aspiring and essentially bourgeois father in a favorable light. The narrator is, thus, a man caught between two worlds; he is part of "the sacrificial generation"—that group of young people expected to trade its own contentment and sense of communality for the ego-satisfaction of the larger black community. Stacy, the former hustler, details the situation.

> Why you came back I'll never know, but you got to make it. Not just for yourself, but for your family, friends, all of us here that ain't never going to make it. How many generations come and gone, how much sacrifice to make one like you? Your life ain't your own boy. Don't seem right do it? You and your kind are the lambs of the sacrifice, when enough of you get out of this place, we'll all get out. (P. 197)

The narrator's problem is one of reconciling black America's hopes and his own individual longings. While he is under the influence of heroin, there is no chance for such a modus vivendi. Moreover, the anguish occasioned by the conflict is so minimized that romantic distortions become normative. In the first half of the novel, therefore, we are presented with a set of values that will not suffice for the second. The narrator is untrustworthy not only from an aesthetic point of view but also from a social point of view. *Utile* and *dulce* blend in the realization that a narcotic stupor produces little truth. What the author introduces as reveries are actually threads of his life that must be grasped if his dilemma is to be meliorated.

This is not to say, of course, that the first half of *Blueschild Baby* is devoid of verisimilitude. The novel is presented as an autobiographical account, and in autobiography there is always a merger of time past with the moment of creation. There are ample clues within the first one hundred pages that the glory and splendor of addiction are mocking treasures. Camaraderie purchased with heroin leads to the erroneous assumption that all black life is a cage overseen by warders in blue. The crouching, bestial posture of the narrator at the beginning of the novel, the cramped holelike den in which he lives, the attempt by Broadway to "take off" his own father, and the misery in Fat's home all give testimony that the drug life is not the actualization of that humane potential the narrator sees in black America. The criteria of truth in autobiography is observed insofar as he allows his feelings of the drugged time to surface, but there is also palpable design in his efforts to correct earlier impressions with the wisdom of hindsight.

The catalytic agent who produces this blend of romanticism and reservation is Nandy. Nandy is, perhaps, the most improbable character in *Blueschild Baby,* but she functions reasonably well as a symbolic heroine. If one tries to invest her with warmth and a beating heart, one is destined to failure. Looked upon as a latter-day Platonic ideal, however, she takes her place beside Laura and Beatrice. She is the light in the dark, the representation of innocent first love, the mother of future generations of clear-sighted young warriors like Tchaka, her firstborn. At the nadir of his descent—having returned to Greenwich Village and the defiling white woman—the narrator encounters Nandy. Love and purposefulness arise in him once again, and he resolves to ascend from hell.

It is at this point that one sees most clearly the novel's orientation. The narrator has gained financial security by confiscating a friend's stash:

> Buy some socks and underclothes and ride downtown feeling like a native who's just spent his first money. Cannot believe I got something in return for it. Something real, that will not vanish like a feeling. I can look at it a week from now and say so much money went there and have something to show for it. (P. 111)

This sounds like the most frugal and Franklinesque character tallying his account books, and when the narrator goes on to set forth paeans for his ideal woman, he sounds like a cross between a Victorian moralist and Eldridge Cleaver in *Soul on Ice.* The hustler's dream of the "big sting" and the American rags-to-riches fantasy come together in the second half of *Blueschild Baby* and produce some inconceivable moments. In order for Nandy to bear her symbolic burden, she must glow with a pubescent radiance; but she is an unwed mother who has lived in the raucous projects all her life. There must be a contrast between Nandy and the narrator, but the attempted

[85]

bifurcation leads to Nandy's improbable assumption that a group of junkies are people gathered to view an accident. For Nandy to serve as a Beatrice, she must come bearing wisdom and an important heritage. While she is from the racist South, however, she still projects the heritage as one diametrically opposed to the oppression of the city, and her didactic passages on jazz and the relationship between black men and white women scarcely rise above clichés.

The problems that Cain encounters in the second half of his novel should not lead one to condemn the ambitiousness of his efforts, for he is attempting to yoke together violently dissimilar assumptions about black American life. The individualistic second half was intended to balance the naturalistic first, and the narrator's confusions were to be mitigated by four factors: financial gain, Nandy, free will, and an autobiographical recall that would enable him to unravel the twisted skein of his former life. Though the money that frees him from the anxieties of the drug life is dubiously obtained, the narrator makes an important assertion when he says that part of the incarcerating force of white America derives from its control of resources. He goes even further when he reveals the students of Brey Prep (a marvelously chosen name) as members of a small group of individuals—narrow in their prejudices and insane in their lifestyle—who control most of these resources. And he is on firm ground when he assesses the black bourgeoisie as a will-less class:

> They went to the same schools, belonged to the same fraternities, clubs and lodges. Went to Sag in summer, attended the same dances and social functions reported faithfully in *Jet, Ebony* and the *Amsterdam*. Where else were their sons and daughters going to find respectable friends and mates, equals among their own color, except in this parody of white society with debs, balls and tuxedoed escorts? And just as far removed and despising of the black mass as the white scene they slavishly aped. (P. 171)

White America not only doles out financial rewards but also sets the style for aspiring black Americans. The narrator's parents have fallen into the trap, and it is only years later that his mother is able to say, "It was a mistake moving to Teaneck" (p. 180). Rather than defining their lives in terms of what they knew best—their own unique culture—his parents have assumed that a move from the city is necessary in order to give their children the benefits of American society, to make them fit for the world in which they are destined to live. The irony is that their spatial and spiritual departure from the black community has left them isolated, ready prey for the bigotry of the suburbs. The narrator comments:

> They're trapped out here, at the mercy of the white mob surrounding them and showing the strain of a prolonged siege. Battle fatigue is setting in. When it comes, they will never reach the safety of the city. They'll be lynched by the white mob. (P. 77)

The social mobility promised by the suburbs strips the black man of his most cherished associations. Like the narrator, he becomes the pawn of that appropriately named divine, Reverend White, and subject to the mentors of a Brey Prep, who carry such Dickensian titles as Mr. Twiceler and Mr. Queen.

During his detoxification, the narrator recollects his past, and always the frenetic movement from the black city—that "drifting slowly but surely" away from himself—is accompanied by visions of the love and camaraderie of youth. The stickball in the street, the festive shopping excursions, the calm of Sunday mornings, and even the unity of the community in times of despair and rebellion (the death of Blue and the resistance of the badman Robles) are set in a positive light. A representative passage illustrates the tone of the whole:

> See the ball rising black out of the canyon's shade, soaring above the buildings into light, pink against blue. Following its flight with my eyes, legs pumping madly, see it fall, lost for a moment returning to shadows, bounding off a building, a fire escape, rolling off and again in space, then caught for an out. The sidewalks and stoops are crowded with men who watch and applaud, recalling themselves in some far off time engaged in similar sport. (Pp. 143-144)

Against such scenes are juxtaposed the father's inconsistencies and confusions, the callousness and pretension of the black middle class, the harried sex affairs of Brey Prep, and the loss of Nandy. The final break comes when Nana's building (in which the great-grandmother has met her death) burns once again. The destruction of the birthplace here, like the fall of the Rochester estate in *Jane Eyre*, signals the end of an historical continuity. As the father and son reclaim Nana's water-soaked possessions, the community itself turns hostile;

[87]

those human statues that were accepted parts of the narrator's youth reveal themselves as scavengers and rogues. Without the significant past as ballast, the narrator drifts into the directionless spheres of the black bourgeoisie. Realizing that he is lost, he seeks to turn again and mistakes "the cheap glamour" of pimps and hustlers for the essence of black life. Though the companions of his innocent days are "tragic figures, comrades of youth, already dead," he follows the addict's route. The results are foreordained: imprisonment for the possession of narcotics and a descent into that hell that opens *Blueschild Baby.*

The second attempt at finding his way from the labyrinth, however, is more successful. He rejects his "acquaintances from the underground," and with Nandy as guide asserts his own free will. With the righteousness of a Reformation convert, he states that the "mad need to punish and destroy ourselves is past, our minds and bodies are needed. We are free if we want to be" (p. 112). And later:

> Thinking of Sun and thousands of others, see the never ending spiral of addiction stretching years before me. Trapped in a prison of my own making which I walk around and carry wherever I go. More secure than bars and gun towers cause there's nothing outside. (P. 126)

Finally, if there is any lingering doubt about the narrator's disposition, there is his fierce struggle with the devil himself:

> Smell the heroin, like metal. Pain in the back, muscles and nerves jumping. Roil around like in a fit. A demon jumps out my head. It is the only way to fight this thing, like it's alive and two-legged. Lay hands on it and throw it off my back. Cannot sit still and let nature take its course. Must take positive action, confront this thing trying to steal my soul. (P. 151)

The pained and distraught sojourner in hell confronts his adversary with Protestant fervor, and the shadow of the ideal woman floats in and out of his consciousness. Surely this is a scene to delight the hearts of holy believers in laissez-faire—particularly when one recognizes that the conversion follows substantial financial gain. Despite the narrator's purchase of African jewelry at the end of the novel, one feels that the cold Puritan leaders of seventeenth-century America would have understood his donning an ersatz scarlet letter better than "the brother in the street."

Yet, in one sense, *Blueschild Baby* represents a synthesis of a

number of black artistic and social concerns. As a fictional autobiography, it stands at the far end of a tradition that begins with the
narrative of Briton Hammon, matures in the work of Frederick
Douglass, expands with James Weldon Johnson's *Autobiography of
an Ex-Colored Man,* and receives acknowledgment during the early
sixties in the works of Claude Brown and Malcolm X. A decade ago,
as the civil rights movement turned northward, black Americans
felt once again a turmoil of the spirit similar to that which accompanied the first declaration of freedom. And men who had come of
age in the city set about recording their individual progress from an
urban bondage to a time of liberation. Removed from the Southern,
agrarian soil that had nurtured their culture, and surrounded by the
allurements of the inner city, both Brown's narrator in *Manchild in
the Promised Land* and Malcolm's in *The Autobiography of Malcolm
X* follow the road of drugs and hustling. The only counter-attractions
for Brown's protagonist seem to be Greenwich Village, a Jewish
adolescent bearing love, and, finally, a scholarship to a black university. *Manchild,* therefore, concludes with a situation like the one that
occasions the suffering of George Cain, and its strategies for
extricating the black soul from a dire condition are quite traditional.

Malcolm's recovered self, on the other hand, adopts methods
that are far from traditional. Rather than a flight to security and
meditation in the white world (Brown's Greenwich Village days),
the narrator's course is composed of a series of educational experiences leading to an existential void. Schooled in the ways of the city
by a number of hustlers, Malcolm sinks to the lowest ebb; he is strung
out on drugs, half insane, and threatened with death by West Indian
Archie and others. Carried to Boston by Shorty, his "homeboy," he
recuperates and establishes the burglary operation that results in his
arrest and imprisonment. Education—in a traditional sense—begins
at this point, and it is shaped by the Black Muslim ideology. On his
release, Malcolm is fully qualified to assume a leadership role. He
understands the mentality and language of urban black America,
and his faith in the correctness of Elijah Muhammad's philosophy is
secure. The crumbling of this faith in the face of devastating reports
on Elijah, and an elucidating trip to Mecca and other sites in Africa
leave Malcolm bewildered. He cannot join the camp of those bour-

geois black leaders whom he has attacked for years, nor can he maintain the militantly anti-white stance of a former time. A Third World perspective, threats on his life, the trials of creating a new movement, and genuine ideological uncertainty seem to have characterized Malcolm just before his death. He faced a task not unlike that of Frederick Douglass when he made his successful bid for freedom. Malcolm, too, confronted the necessity of creating being out of dehumanization and despair; he, too, sought to extract a fruitful and unfettered essence from a bleak existence. The instruments at hand for Douglass were his own fierce will and the survival values of a Southern, black, agrarian culture. For Malcolm, there was a somewhat shaken will and the assets of a Northern, black, urban culture plagued by crime and divided in its strategies for survival. He went as far as any man could, given these conditions.

Blueschild Baby begins at the void before which Malcolm magnificently faltered and projects beyond this abyss to a new dawning of the black spirit. Although there is a good deal of that confusion which beset Malcolm—the fall before the temptation of drugs and the Protestant, middle-class fervor that has led critics to compare Malcolm's work with Benjamin Franklin's—there is also a candid and laudatory delineation of black urban culture. For Cain's narrator, the black inner city is not a domain populated solely by the spectacular criminal and the wretched of the earth. It is also a place where extended black families reside, where oral historians give valuable lessons in the continuity of a culture, and where old men with long memories bestow tenderness on the young. Moreover, there is in this domain a growing black consciousness. Committed men post warnings to pimps and hustlers to leave the community; all over Harlem men show their regard for Nandy's beauty, and, through her symbolic role, the culture's; and the Newark riot—that tangible manifestation of a rebellious spirit—governs much of the action. Presumably, this building self-awareness of the larger community both motivates and mirrors the course of the narrator's ascent. The strong impression that he achieves his liberation alone is modified by those developmental autobiographical scenes that make one feel the weight, joy, and importance of his childhood in the city. And the individualism is further qualified by the life-and-times aspects of the book: the actions and resolves that demonstrate a genuine concern with a framework of objective events. Rather than punching the holes of his subjective experience through this frame (as Stephen Spender phrased it), George Cain makes it a moving force in his story.

Blueschild Baby, then, reflects the divided loyalties and misdirection that convulsed the black freedom struggle of the sixties. And the temper and pattern of the narrative are at points disastrously akin to those in the Horatio Alger stories. But the lack of certainty and the hopelessly white, middle-class efforts poured forth by men and women with dark skins were only part of the story. There were also attempts at definition and a celebration of that new locus of black culture, the inner city. Its surface manifestations held some writers in thrall; they could not see beyond criminality. Cain's narrator, however, captures the essentials. The center of value is not the soil of the South, as it was for Jean Toomer's sensitive and accomplished narrator in *Cane*. It is the glistening asphalt and teeming tenements of a new frontier. The sixties constituted a period in which claims were staked. In the seventies, there are authors like George Cain who strive to illustrate the spirit necessary for continued growth.

Out of a city existence, *Blueschild Baby* brings essence; out of nothingness, or the void left by Malcolm's autobiography, it creates being. Again one has that dream at the root of the American collective unconscious—the reverie of a "new man" achieving an ideal community—and Richard Wright's assertion that the black man is America's metaphor is once more confirmed.

Conclusion

AND he said to me: 'It is because thou piercest the dark from too far off that thou strayest in thy fancy, and if thou reach the place thou shalt see plainly how much the sense is deceived by distance; push on, therefore, with more speed.' " This injunction from one poet to another captures the drive that one feels in the work of Paul Laurence Dunbar, James Weldon Johnson, Jean Toomer, Gwendolyn Brooks, Ralph Ellison, Malcolm X, and George Cain. Having death and slavery ever present before their eyes, they have still sought the secret of the stars. They have illumined what the African writer Léopold Sédar Senghor calls the spirit of a civilization by providing an alternative and essential vision. Writers like Dunbar and Toomer delved beneath the surface darkness and the pain of long suffering to discover the rhythmic pulses of the folk, and Gwendolyn Brooks has distilled the multifaceted flow of black life into the harmonies of verse. The towering and analytic works of Johnson and Ellison laid out the framework of a culture, giving back to the reader not only the recognizable bleakness but also the oftentimes concealed brightness and singularity. Malcolm stands at the threshold of a modern consciousness, and George Cain is one of the most talented black writers who have attempted to move from a vague design and the barest beginnings to the new structure itself.

But the overall intent of this volume has not been to assert that things are never as bad as they seem, or some other equally inept cliché. The burdens of the black situation are real and omnipresent in America, and mournful numbers are frequently as appropriate as any semblance of optimism. The evocation of historical misery, in other words, keeps one aware of the struggle yet to be waged and can also lead to that transmutation of suffering into historicity that constitutes a broader humanism. And yet, one can become so embroiled in the political battles of one's own era that one forgets the real contributions of those poets of the past and present who have kept the resplendent always in view, who have broken through the somber layers of their social and artistic situation to articulate a stirring account of black dignity and achievement. Such estrangement or forgetfulness can prove disastrous, because finally we have no one but our poets to apprehend the pressing necessity of change. When they give back to us—as James Baldwin has stated it—our history in a bearable form, they also lead the transformations that make for a new day. They stand upon the hill with pen (and sword) in hand, beckoning us toward the light.

Notes

Chapter II

1. Winthrop Jordan, *White Over Black* (Baltimore: Penguin Books, 1969), p. 109.
2. Booker T. Washington, *Up From Slavery,* in *Three Negro Classics,* ed. John Hope Franklin (New York: Avon Books, 1969), p. 81.
3. W. E. B. Du Bois, *Dusk of Dawn* (New York: Schocken Books, 1968), p. 143.
4. Quoted from *The Book of Negro Folklore*, ed. Langston Hughes and Arna Bontemps (New York: Dodd, Mead & Company, 1958), p. 13.
5. Frederick Douglass, *Narrative of the Life of Frederick Douglass, An American Slave, Written by Himself* (New York: Signet Books, 1968).
6. Jean Paul Sartre, *L'Existentialisme est un Humanisme* (Paris: Les Editions Nagel, 1946).
7. Albert Camus, *The Myth of Sisyphus and Other Essays* (New York: Alfred A. Knopf, 1955).

Chapter III

1. Northrop Frye, "All Ye Know on Earth," *The Well-Tempered Critic* (Bloomington: Indiana University Press, 1963), pp. 134-35.
2. Ralph Ellison, *Invisible Man* (New York: Random House, 1952), p. 307.

3. William C. Fischer, "The Aggregate Man in Jean Toomer's *Cane*," *Studies in the Novel* III (1971): 191. The writer also points out the communal nature of the experiences and the autobiographical impulse operative in both works.

4. James Weldon Johnson, *The Autobiography of an Ex-Colored Man,* in *Three Negro Classics,* ed. John Hope Franklin (New York: Avon Books, 1969), pp. 394-95. All citations refer to this edition.

5. W. E. B. Du Bois, *The Souls of Black Folk,* in *Three Negro Classics,* ed. John Hope Franklin (New York: Avon Books, 1969), p. 214.

6. James Weldon Johnson, *Along This Way* (New York: Viking Press, 1968), p. 203.

7. Jean Toomer, "Song of the Son," *Cane* (New York: Harper & Row, Publishers, 1969), p. 21.

8. In *The Negro Novel in America* (New Haven: Yale University Press, 1965), p. 47, Robert Bone states that "moral cowardice" constitutes "the theme that runs persistently throughout" *The Autobiography of an Ex-Colored Man.* This, however, seems a superficial reading if one considers the protagonist's own words. If one takes into consideration the amoral white universe in which the narrator is set, the proposition becomes absurd.

9. Frederick Douglass, *Narrative of the Life of Frederick Douglass,* p. 123.

10. For those bothered by this spatial consideration and genuinely interested in images of vision in *Invisible Man,* there is Charles I. Glicksberg's "The Symbolism of Vision," *Southwest Review* XXXIX (1954): 259-65.

11. Stewart Lillard's "Ellison's Ambitious Scope in *Invisible Man,*" *English Journal* LVIII: 833-39, and Richard Kostelanetz's "The Politics of Ellison's Booker: *Invisible Man* as Symbolic History," *Chicago Review* XIX (1967): 5-26, offer further discussions of the role of black American history in Ellison's novel.

12. Ralph Ellison, "Richard Wright's Blues," *Shadow and Act* (New York: New American Library, 1966), p. 90.

13. William J. Schafer, "Ralph Ellison and the Birth of the Anti-Hero," *Critique* X (1968): 82.

Chapter IV

1. Paul Laurence Dunbar, *The Complete Poems of Paul Laurence Dunbar* (New York: Dodd, Mead & Company, 1913), p. vii.

2. Victor Lawson, *Paul Laurence Dunbar Critically Examined* (Washington, D.C.: Associated Publishers, 1941), p. 139.

3. Saunders Redding, "The Negro Writer and American Literature," in *Anger and Beyond,* ed. Herbert Hill (New York: Harper & Row, Publishers, 1968), pp. 1-2.

4. T. S. Eliot, "William Blake," *Selected Essays* (New York: Harcourt, Brace and Company, 1950), pp. 275-80.

5. Sterling Brown, *Negro Poetry and Drama* (New York: Atheneum Publishers, 1969), pp. 82-92.

Chapter V

1. Imamu Amiri Baraka (LeRoi Jones), "The Myth of a 'Negro Literature'," *Home: Social Essays* (New York: William Morrow, 1966), pp. 105-15.

2. Etheridge Knight, "To Gwendolyn Brooks," *Poems From Prison* (Detroit: Broadside Press, 1968), p. 30.

3. Gwendolyn Brooks, *Selected Poems* (New York: Harper & Row, Publishers, 1963), p. 3. All citations of the poetry of Gwendolyn Brooks in my text refer to this edition.

4. David Littlejohn, *Black on White: A Critical Survey of Writing by American Negroes* (New York: Viking Press, 1969), pp. 89-94.

Chapter VI

1. William Stanley Braithwaite, "The Negro in American Literature," *The New Negro*, ed. Alain Locke (New York: Atheneum Publishers, 1968), pp. 29-44.

2. Langston Hughes, "The Negro Artist and the Racial Mountain," *Amistad I* (New York: Random House, 1970), pp. 301-5. [First published in *The Nation*, June 23, 1926.]

3. Thurman lived a flamboyant life in New York and Hollywood from 1925 to 1934. He died of alcoholism and tuberculosis on New York's Welfare Island. For a brief biographical sketch, see Dorothy West's "Elephant Dance," *Black World* XX (November, 1970): 77-85.

4. Claude McKay, *A Long Way from Home* (New York: Harcourt Brace & World, 1970). McKay's autobiography describes his travels during the twenties and contains his reflections on the Harlem Renaissance.

5. For accounts of the Harlem Renaissance in general and the careers of Cullen and Hughes during the twenties, see Langston Hughes's *The Big Sea* (New York: Hill and Wang, 1968) and Blanche E. Ferguson's *Countee Cullen and the Negro Renaissance* (New York: Dodd, Mead & Company, 1966). Hughes's autobiography was first published in 1940.

6. Arna Bontemps, "Introduction," *Cane* (New York: Harper & Row, Publishers, 1969), p. x.

7. Jean Toomer, *Cane* (New York: Harper & Row, Publishers, 1969), p. 1. All citations of *Cane* in my text refer to this edition.

8. I am indebted to Professor James Nash for his suggestion concerning duality in *Cane,* and I cannot thank him enough for reading my manuscript and contributing his editorial skills toward its completion.

9. William J. Goede, "Jean Toomer's Ralph Kabnis: Portrait of the Negro Artist as a Young Man," *Phylon* XXX (1969): 75. In *The Negro Novel* (New Haven: Yale University Press, 1965), p. 83, Bone calls Becky's house, "a cabin built by community guilt."

10. Georges Devereux, *Essais d'ethnopsychiatrie générale,* translated by Henri Gobard (Paris: Gallimard, 1970), p. 18. An entire section of Devereux's first chapter (pp. 14-31) is devoted to what he terms *Les Désordres Sacrés (Chamaniques),* and I wish to thank Mme. Yvette Rude of Vincennes University for calling my attention to the work.

11. Bontemps, "Introduction," *Cane,* pp. xii-xiii.

12. Quoted by Alain Locke in "Negro Youth Speaks," *The New Negro,* p. 51.

13. In "The Aggregate Man in Jean Toomer's *Cane,*" *Studies in the Novel* III (1971), pp. 190-213, William C. Fischer says: "The moving force behind the abuse and pain endured by Toomer's women is in fact the relentless debilitation of the black man in the white rural South."

14. For a further discussion of this theme and its ramifications, see my essay, "Freedom and Apocalypse: A thematic approach to Black Expression," *Long Black Song: Essays in Black American Literature and Culture* (Charlottesville: University Press of Virginia, 1972), pp. 42-57.

15. Edward E. Waldron, "The Search for Identity in Jean Toomer's 'Esther'," *CLA Journal* XIV (1971): 277.

16. A professional individual for whom Toomer had great aversion: "There seems to have been no shop-keepers or shysters among us," he said in his letter to the editors of the *Liberator* in 1922 (quoted from Bontemps, "Introduction," *Cane,* p. ix). In "Kabnis," there appears not only the unfavorable portrayal of the businessman Halsey but also the protagonist's bitterly cynical denunciation: "Hence, what comes from Him is ugly. Lynchers and business men, and that cockroach Hanby, especially" (p. 162).

17. Fischer, "The Aggregate Man in Jean Toomer's *Cane,*" p. 200.

18. In David Walker's *Appeal* (1829), Frederick Douglass's *Narrative of the Life of Frederick Douglass* (1845), and William Wells Brown's *Narrative of William Wells Brown, A Fugitive Slave* (1847), there are innumerable passages condemning supposedly Christian whites who enslave and brutalize black Americans.

19. In "Jean Toomer's Black Authenticity," *Black World* XX (1970): 70-76, Clifford Mason comments aptly that Toomer realized that "the emptiness of our black lives has been due as much to our being psychological mimics as it has been to the accumulation of what the white man has wrought."

20. James Edwin Howard takes this same line of analysis in his "Structure and Search in Jean Toomer's *Cane*," (unpublished manuscript, University of Virginia, 1970), p. 3.

21. Goede, "Jean Toomer's Ralph Kabnis."

22. Darwin T. Turner, "Jean Toomer's *Cane*," *Negro Digest* XVIII (January, 1969): 57.

23. Bone, *Negro Novel in America*, p. 84.

24. Imamu Amiri Baraka (LeRoi Jones), "The dance," *The Dead Lecturer* (New York: Grove Press, 1964), p. 71.

25. Bone, Fischer, and Turner all see the protagonist of "Kabnis" as a failure in his quest for meaning. And in "A Key to the Poems in *Cane*," *CLA Journal* XIV (March, 1971): 251-58, Bernard Bell describes him in the same terms.

26. Bontemps, "Introduction," *Cane*, p. xiii.

27. Goede, "Jean Toomer's Ralph Kabnis, p. 85.

28. Eugenia W. Collier, "Heritage From Harlem," *Black World* XX (November, 1970): 54. For further discussion of the folk influence during the Harlem Renaissance see the introduction to "The Awakening of the Twenties" and "Black American Literature: An Overview" in my *Black Literature in America* (New York: McGraw-Hill, 1971).

Chapter VII

1. George Cain, *Blueschild Baby* (New York: McGraw-Hill Book Company, 1970), p. 1. All citations of *Blueschild Baby* in my text refer to this edition.

2. W. E. B. Du Bois, "Of the Coming of John," *The Souls of Black Folk*, in *Three Negro Classics*, ed. John Hope Franklin (New York: Avon Books, 1969) pp. 363-77.

Selected Bibliography of Criticism

I. Gwendolyn Brooks

Beja, Morris. "It Must Be Important." *Antioch Review* XXIV (Fall, 1964): 323-36.

Bird, G. Leonard. "Gwendolyn Brooks: Educator Extraordinaire." *Discourse* XII: 158-66.

Crockett, Jacqueline. "An Essay on Gwendolyn Brooks." *Negro History Bulletin* XIX (November, 1955): 37-39.

Davis, Arthur P. "The Black-and-Tan Motif in the Poetry of Gwendolyn Brooks." *CLA Journal* VI (December, 1962): 90-97.

———"Gwendolyn Brooks: Poet of the Unheroic." *CLA Journal* VII (December, 1963): 114-25.

Furman, Marva Riley. "Gwendolyn Brooks: The 'Unconditioned' Poet." *CLA Journal* XVII, i. (1973): 1-10.

Gayle, Addison, Jr. "Making Beauty From Racial Anxiety." *New York Times Book Review,* January 2, 1972, p. 4.

Hansell, William H. "Aestheticism Versus Political Militancy in Gwendolyn Brooks' 'The Chicago Picasso' and 'The Wall'." *CLA Journal* XVII, i (1973): 11-15.

Hudson, Clenora F. "Racial Themes in the Poetry of Gwendolyn Brooks." *CLA Journal* XVII, i (1973): 16-20.

Kent, George. "The Poetry of Gwendolyn Brooks, Part I." *Black World* XX, xi (1971): 30-43.

———— "The Poetry of Gwendolyn Brooks, Part II." *Black World* XX, xii (1971): p. 36.

Lee, Don L. "The Achievement of Gwendolyn Brooks." *The Black Scholar* III (Summer, 1972): 32-41.

Littlejohn, David. *Black on White: A Critical Survey of Writings by American Negroes.* New York: Viking Press, 1969.

Loff, John N. "Gwendolyn Brooks: A Bibliography." *CLA Journal* XVII, i (1973): 21-32.

Ray, David. "Brooks, Gwendolyn." In *Contemporary Poets of the English Language,* Edited by Rosalie Murphy and James Vinson, pp. 139-41. New York: St. Martin's Press, 1970.

Shands, Annette Oliver. "Gwendolyn Brooks as Novelist." *Black World* XXII (June, 1973): 22-30.

Stavros, George. "An Interview with Gwendolyn Brooks." *Contemporary Literature* XI (1971): 1-20.

Walker, Margaret. "New Poets." In *Black Expression,* edited by Addison Gayle, Jr. New York: Weybright and Talley, 1968.

II. Paul Laurence Dunbar

Achille, Louis T. "Paul Laurence Dunbar: Poète Nègre." *Revue Anglo-Americain* XII (1934): 504-19.

Arnold, Edward F. "Some Personal Reminiscences of Paul Laurence Dunbar." *Journal of Negro History* XVII (1932): 400-08.

Brawley, Benjamin. "Dunbar Thirty Years After." *Southern Workman* LIX (1930): 189-91.

————*Paul Laurence Dunbar, Poet of His People.* Port Washington, New York: Kennikat Press, 1936.

Burch, Charles E. "Dunbar's Poetry in Literary English." *Southern Workman* L (1921): 469-73.

Butcher, Philip. "Mutual Appreciation: Dunbar and Cable." *CLA Journal* II (1958): 101-02.

Cunningham, Virginia. *Paul Laurence Dunbar and His Song.* 1947. Reprint. New York: Biblo and Tannen Booksellers and Publishers, 1969.

Daniel, T. W. "Paul Laurence Dunbar and the Democratic Ideal." *Negro History Bulletin* VI (1943): 206-08.

Fox, Allan B. "Behind the Mask: Paul Laurence Dunbar's Poetry in Literary English." *Texas Quarterly* XIV, ii. (1971): 7-19.

Gayle, Addison, Jr. *Oak and Ivy: A Biography of Paul Laurence Dunbar.* New York: Doubleday & Company, 1971.

Gloster, Hugh M. *Negro Voices in American Fiction.* Chapel Hill: University of North Carolina Press, 1948.

Gould, Jean. *That Dunbar Boy.* New York: Dodd, Mead & Company, 1958.

Hudson, Gossie Harold. "Paul Laurence Dunbar: Dialect et la Négritude." *Phylon* XXXIV, iii (1973): 236-47.

Larson, Charles L. "The Novels of Paul Laurence Dunbar." *Phylon* XXIX, iii. (1968): 257-71.

Lawson, Victor. *Paul Laurence Dunbar Critically Examined.* Washington, D. C.: Associated Publishers, 1941.

Redding, Saunders. *To Make A Poet Black.* Chapel Hill: University of North Carolina Press, 1939.

Turner, Darwin. "Paul Laurence Dunbar: The Rejected Symbol." *Journal of Negro History* LII (1967): 1-13.

Wagner, Jean. *Black Poets of the U.S.: From Paul Laurence Dunbar to Langston Hughes.* Urbana: University of Illinois Press, 1973.

Walker, Allen. "Paul Dunbar, A Study in Genius." *Psychoanalytic Review* XXV (January, 1938).

III. Ralph Ellison

Baumback, Jonathan. "Nightmare of a Native Son: Ellison's *Invisible Man.*" *Criticism* VI (1963): 48-65.

Bell, J.D. "Ellison's *Invisible Man.*" *Explicator* XXIX (1970): Item 19.

Benoit, Bernard, and Michel Fabre. "A Bibliography of Ralph Ellison's Published Writings." *Studies in Black Literature* II, iii (1971): 25-28.

Bloch, Alice. "Sight Imagery in *Invisible Man.*" *English Journal* LV (1966): p. 1019.

Bluestein, Gene. "The Blues as Literary Theme." *Massachusetts Review* VIII (1967): 593-617.

Bone, Robert A. *The Negro Novel In America.* New Haven: Yale University Press, 1965.

——— "Ralph Ellison and the Uses of Imagination." In *Anger and Beyond,* edited by Herbert Hill, pp. 86-111. New York: Harper & Row, Publishers, 1969. Reprinted in *TriQuarterly* VI, pp. 39-54.

CLA Journal XIII, iii (1970). Ralph Ellison Special Number (Archie D. Sanders, "Odysseus in Black: An Analysis of the Structure of *Invisible Man,*" 217-28; Lawrence J. Clipper, "Folkloric and Mythic Elements in *Invisible Man,*" 229-41; Eleanor R. Wilner, "The Invisible Thread: Identity and Nonentity in *Invisible Man,*" 242-57; Darwin Turner, "Sight in *Invisible Man,*" 258-64; George E. Kent, "Ralph Ellison and the Afro-American Folk and Cultural Tradition," 265-76; Phyllis R. Klotman, "The Running Man as Metaphor in Ellison's *Invisible Man,*" 277-88; Lloyd W. Brown, "Ralph Ellison's Exhorters: The Role of Rhetoric in *Invisible Man,*" 289-303; Floyd R. Horowitz, "An Experimental Confession From a Reader of *Invisible Man,*" 304-14; Thomas LeClair, "The Blind Leading the Blind: Wright's *Native Son* and a Brief Reference to Ellison's *Invisible Man,*" 315-20.)

Clarke, John H. "The Visible Dimensions of *Invisible Man.*" *Black World* XX, ii (1970): 27-30.

Collier, Eugenia W. "The Nightmare Truth of an Invisible Man." *Black World* XX, ii (1970): 12-19.

Corry, John. "Profile of an American Novelist: A White View of Ralph Ellison." *Black World* XX, ii (1970): 116-25.

Covo, Jacqueline. "Ralph Waldo Ellison: Bibliographic Essays and Finding List of American Criticism 1952-64." *CLA Journal* XV (1971): 171-96.

——— "Ralph Ellison in France: Bibliographic Essays and Checklist of French Criticism, 1954-71." *CLA Journal* XVI, iv (1973): 519-26.

Deutsch, Leonard J. "Ralph Waldo Ellison and Ralph Waldo Emerson: A Shared Moral Vision." *Phylon* XVI (1956): 159-78.

Emanuel, James A. "The Invisible Men of American Literature." *Books Abroad* XXXVI (1963): 391-94.

Fass, Barbara. "Rejection of Paternalism: Hawthorne's 'My Kinsman Major Molineux' and Ellison's *Invisible Man.*" *CLA Journal* XIV (1971: 317-24.

Ford, Nick A. "The Ambivalence of Ralph Ellison." *Black World* XX, ii (1970): 5-9.

Geller, Allen. "An Interview with Ralph Ellison." *Tamarack Review* no. 32, pp. 3-24.

Gibson, Donald B., ed. *Five Black Writers: Essays on Wright, Ellison, Baldwin, Hughes and LeRoi Jones.* New York: New York University Press, 1970.

Glicksberg, Charles I. "The Symbolism of Vision." *Southwest Review* XXXIX (1954): 259-65.

Greene, Maxine, "Against Invisibility." *College English* XXX (1969): 430-36.

Griffin, Edward M. "Notes from a Clean, Well-Lighted Place: Ralph Ellison's *Invisible Man.*" *Twentieth Century Literature* XIV (1969): 129-44.

Hassan, Ihab. "The Novel of Outrage: A Minority Voice in Postwar American Fiction." *American Scholar* XXXIV (1965): 239-53.

——— *Radical Innocence.* Princeton: Princeton University Press, 1961.

Hays, Peter L. "The Incest Theme In *Invisible Man.*" *Western Humanities Review* XXIII (1969): 335-39.

Horowitz, Floyd Ross. "The Enigma of Ralph Ellison's Intellectual Man." *CLA Journal* VII (1963): 126-32.

Howard, David C. "Points in Defense of Ellison's *Invisible Man.*" *Notes on Contemporary Literature* II (1971): 13-14.

Howe, Irving. "A Reply to Ralph Ellison." *The New Leader* XLVII (1964): 12-22.

Isaacs, Harold R. "Five Black Writers and Their African Ancestors." *Phylon* XXI (1960): 317-36.

Kaiser, Ernest. "A Critical Look at Ellison's Fiction and at Social and Literary Criticism by and about the Author." *Black World* XX, ii (1970): 53-59, 81-97.

Klein, Marcus. "Ralph Ellison." *After Alienation.* Cleveland: World Publishing Company, 1964.

Kostelanetz, Richard. "The Politics of Ellison's Booker: *Invisible Man* as Symbolic History." *Chicago Review* XIX, ii (1967): 5-26.

——— "Ralph Ellison: Novelist as Brown-Skinned Aristocrat." *Shenandoah* XX, iv (1969): 56-77.

Lee, Robert A. "Sight and Mask: Ralph Ellison's *Invisible Man.*" *Negro American Literature Forum* IV (1970): 22-23.

Lehan, Richard. "The Strange Silence of Ralph Ellison." *California English Journal* I, ii (1965): 63-68.

Lieber, Todd M. "Ralph Ellison and the Metaphor of Invisibility in Black Literary Tradition." *American Quarterly* XXIV, i (March, 1972): 86-100.

Lieberman, Marcia R. "Moral Innocents: Ellison's *Invisible Man* and *Candide.*" *CLA Journal* XV (1971): 64-79.

Ludington, Charles T., Jr. "Protest and Anti-protest: Ralph Ellison." *Southern Humanities Review* IV (1970): 31-39.

Margolies, Edward. *Native Sons: A Critical Study of Twentieth Century Negro American Authors.* Philadelphia: J. B. Lippincott Company, 1968.

Mason, Clifford. "Ralph Ellison and the Underground Man." *Black World* XX, iii (1970): 20-26.

Mengeling, Marvin E. "Whitman and Ellison: Older Symbols in a Modern Mainstream." *Walt Whitman Review* XII (1966): 67-70.

Moorer, Frank E. and Lugene Bailey. "A Selected Check List of Material by and about Ralph Ellison." *Black World* XX, iii (1970): 126-30.

Neal, Larry. "Ellison's Zoot Suit." *Black World* XX, ii (1970): 31-52.

Nichols, William W. "Ralph Ellison's Black American Scholar." *Phylon* XXXI (1970): 70-75.

O'Daniel, Therman B. "The Image of Man as Portrayed by Ralph Ellison." *CLA Journal* X (1967): 277-84.

Olderman, Raymond M. "Ralph Ellison's Blues and *Invisible Man.*" *Wisconsin Studies in Contemporary Literature* VII (1966): 142-59.

Radford, Frederick L. "The Journey Towards Castration: Interracial Sexual Stereotypes in Ellison's *Invisible Man.*" *Journal of American Studies* IV (1970): 227-31.

Reilly, John M., ed. *Twentieth Century Interpretations of* Invisible Man: *A Collection of Critical Essays.* Englewood Cliffs, N.J.: Prentice-Hall, 1970.

Rodnon, Stewart. "Ralph Ellison's *Invisible Man:* Six Tentative Approaches." *CLA Journal* XII (1969): 211-56.

Rollins, Ronald G. "Ellison's *Invisible Man*." *Explicator* XXX (1971): Item 22.

Rovit, Earl H. "Ralph Ellison and the American Comic Tradition." *Wisconsin Studies in Contemporary Literature* I (1960): 34-42.

Schafer, William J. "Irony From Underground: Satiric Elements in *Invisible Man*." *Satire Newsletter* VII (1969): 22-29.

——— "Ralph Ellison and the Birth of the Anti-Hero." *Critique: Studies in Modern Fiction* X, ii (1968): 81-93.

Thompson, James; Lennox Raphael, and Steve Cannon. "A Very Stern Discipline: An Interview with Ralph Ellison." *Harper's* CCXXXIV (March): 76-95.

Trimmer, Joseph A. *A Casebook on Ralph Ellison's* Invisible Man. New York: Thomas Y. Crowell Co., 1972.

Waghmare, J.M. "Invisibility and the American Negro: Ralph Ellison's *Invisible Man*." *Quest* LIX (1968): 23-30.

Walling, William. " 'Art' and 'Protest': Ralph Ellison's *Invisible Man* Twenty Years After." *Phylon* XXXIV, ii (1973): 120-34.

———"Ralph Ellison's *Invisible Man*: 'It Goes A Long Way Back. Some Twenty years'." *Phylon* XXXIV, ii (1973): 4-16.

Warren, Robert Penn. "The Unity of Experience." *Commentary* XXXIX, (1965): 91-96.

Williams, John A. "Ralph Ellison and *Invisible Man*: Their Place in American Letters." *Black World* XX, ii (1970): 10-11.

IV. James Weldon Johnson

Adelman, Lynn. "A Study of James Weldon Johnson." *Journal of Negro History* LII (1967): 128-45.

Aptheker, Herbert. "Du Bois on James Weldon Johnson." *Journal of Negro History* LII (1967): 224-27.

Avery, William A. "James Weldon Johnson: American Negro of Distinction." *School and Society* XLVIII (1938): 291-94.

Bronz, Stephen H. *Roots of Negro Racial Consciousness.* Roslyn Heights, N.Y.: Libra, 1964.

Collier, Eugenia. "James Weldon Johnson: Mirror of Change." *Phylon* XXI (1960): 351-59.

Fleming, Robert E. "Contemporary Themes in Johnson's *Autobiography of an Ex-Colored Man*." *Negro American Literature Forum* IV (1970): 120.

——— "Irony as a Key to Johnson's *Autobiography of an Ex-Colored Man*." *American Literature* XLIII (1971): 83-96.

Garrett, Marvin P. "Early Recollections and Structural Irony in *The Autobiography of an Ex-Colored Man*." *Critique: Studies in Modern Fiction* XIII, iii (1971): 5-14.

Jackson, Miles, Jr. "James Weldon Johnson." *Black World* XIX, viii (1970): 32-34.

Kostelanetz, Richard. "The Politics of Passing: The Fiction of James Weldon Johnson." *Negro American Literature Forum* III (1969): 22.

Levy, Eugene. *James Weldon Johnson: Black Leader, Black Voice.* Edited by John H. Franklin. Negro American Biography and Autobiography Series. Chicago: University of Chicago Press, 1973.

——— "Ragtime and Race Pride: The Career of James Weldon Johnson." *Journal of Popular Culture* I (1968): 357-70.

Long, Richard A. "A Weapon of my Song: The Poetry of James Weldon Johnson." *Phylon* XXXIII (1971): 374-82.

Tarry, Ellen. *Young Jim: The Early Years of James Weldon Johnson.* New York: Dodd, Mead & Company, 1967.

Tate, E. C. "Sentiment and Horse Sense: James Weldon Johnson's Style." *Negro History Bulletin* XXV (April, 1962): 152-54.

V. Malcolm X

Berthoff, Warner. "Witness and Testament: Two Contemporary Classics." *New Literary History* II (1971): 311-27.

Clarke, John Henrik. *Malcolm X: The Man and His Times.* New York: Macmillan Company, 1969.

Demarest, David P. *"The Autobiography of Malcolm X:* Beyond Didacticism." *CLA Journal* XVI, ii (1972): 179-87.

Hoyt, Charles A. "The Five Faces of Malcolm X." *Negro American Literature Forum* IV (1970): 107-12.

Ohmann, Carol. *"The Autobiography of Malcolm X:* A Revolutionary Use of the Franklin Tradition." *American Quarterly* XXII (1970): 131-49.

Warren, R. P. "Malcolm X: Mission and Meaning." *Yale Review* LVI (December, 1966): 161-71.

VI. Jean Toomer

Bontemps, Arna. "The Negro Renaissance: Jean Toomer and the Harlem Writers of the 1920's." In *Anger and Beyond,* edited by Herbert Hill, pp. 20-36. New York: Harper & Row, Publishers, 1969.

Bronz, Stephen H. *Roots of Negro Racial Consciousness, the 1920s: Three Harlem Renaissance Authors.* Roslyn, N.Y.: Libra, 1964.

Chapman, Abraham. "The Harlem Renaissance in Literary History." *CLA Journal* XI (1967): 38-58.

Chase, Patricia. "The Women in *Cane.*" *CLA Journal* XIV (1971): 259-73.

Duncan, Bowie. "Jean Toomer's *Cane:* A Modern Black Oracle." *CLA Journal* XV (1972): 323-33.

Durham, Frank, ed. *The Merrill Studies in Cane*. Columbus, Ohio: Charles E. Merrill Books, 1971.

Farrison, William Edward. "Jean Toomer's *Cane* Again." *CLA Journal* XV (1972): 303-22.

Frank, Waldo. Foreword to *Cane*, by Jean Toomer. New York: University Place Press, 1967.

Fullinwider, P. S. "Jean Toomer: Lost Generation or Negro Renaissance?" *Phylon* XXVII (1966): 396-403.

Huggins, Nathan Irvin. *Harlem Renaissance*. New York: Oxford University Press, 1971.

Hughes, Langston. "The Twenties: Harlem and its Negritude." *African Forum* I (1966): 10-20.

Innes, Catherine L. "The Unity of Jean Toomer's *Cane*." *CLA Journal* XV (1972): 306-22.

Keller, Frances Richardson. "The Harlem Literary Renaissance." *North American Review* V (1968): 29-34.

Lieber, Todd. "Design and Movement in *Cane*." *CLA Journal* XIII (1969): 35-50.

Scruggs, Charles W. "A Mark of Cain and the Redemption of Art: A Study in Theme and Structure of Jean Toomer's *Cane*." *American Literature* XLIV (1972): 276-91.

Turner, Darwin. *In a Minor Chord*. Carbondale: Southern Illinois University Press, 1971.

Watkins, Patricia. "Is There a Unifying Theme in *Cane*?" *CLA Journal* XV (1972): 303-22.

VII. Richard Wright

Abcarian, Richard. *Richard Wright's* Native Son, *A Critical Handbook*. Belmont, California: Wadsworth Publishing Company, 1970.

Baker, Houston A., Jr., ed. *Twentieth Century Interpretations of* Native Son. Englewood Cliffs, N.J.: Prentice-Hall, 1972. (Richard Wright, "How 'Bigger' Was Born," 21-47; James Baldwin, "Many Thousands Gone," 48-62; Irving Howe, "Black Boys and Native Sons," 63-70; Robert A. Bone, "Richard Wright," 71-81; Dan McCall, "The Bad Nigger," 82-90; George E. Kent, "Richard Wright: Blackness and the Adventure of Western Culture," 91-95; Donald B. Gibson, "Wright's Invisible Native Son," 96-108; Dorothy Canfield Fisher, "Introduction to the First Edition," 109-11; Malcolm Cowley, "Richard Wright: The Case of Bigger Thomas," 112-14; Nelson Algren, "Remembering Richard Wright," 115-16.)

Brignano, Carl. *Richard Wright: An Introduction to the Man and His Work*. Pittsburgh: University of Pittsburgh Press, 1970.

Selected Bibliography of Criticism

Bryer, Jackson R. "Richard Wright (1908-1960): A Selected Checklist of Criticism." *Wisconsin Studies in Contemporary Literature* I (1960): 22-33.

Burgum, Edwin Berry. "The Promise of Democracy in Richard Wright's *Native Son*." In *The Novel and the World's Dilemma*. New York: Russell and Russell, 1963.

Creekmore, Herbert. "Social Factors in *Native Son*." *University Review* VIII (1941): 136-43.

Ellison, Ralph. "The World and the Jug." In *Shadow and Act,* pp. 115-47. New York: Random House, 1964.

Emanuel, James A. "Fever and Feeling: Notes on the Imagery of *Native Son*." *Negro Digest* XVIII (1968): 16-26.

Fabre, Michel. *The Unfinished Quest of Richard Wright*. New York: William Morrow and Company, 1973.

Gibson, Donald B. "Richard Wright: A Bibliographical Essay." *CLA Journal* XII (1969): 360-65.

Kinnamon, Keneth. "*Native Son:* The Personal, Social, and Political Background." *Phylon* XXX (1969): 66-72.

Margolies, Edward. *The Art of Richard Wright*. Carbondale: Southern Illinois University Press, 1969.

Redding, Saunders. "The Alien Land of Richard Wright." In *Soon One Morning*, edited by Herbert Hill, pp. 50-59. New York: Alfred A. Knopf, 1965.

Scott, Nathan A. "Search for Beliefs: Fiction of Richard Wright." *University of Kansas City Review* XXIII (1956): 19-24, 131-38.

pb

AUG 0 1 1988